FAILURES ARE THE PILLARS TO SUCCESS

PRANJAL BORKAR

Made with ♥ on the Notion Press Platform
www.notionpress.com

Contents

I
Introduction

I know that probably everyone of you, is aware with the word "FAILURE". Always remember the world you see with your beautifull eyes there are certain minds which are very charming and beautiful from inside so does it means that the once who are charming and beautiful they dont make any mistake they have'nt failed in there way of life . One thing I can tell one thing for sure that whatever we do it has some or any other reason as we humans are selfish ,do you agree for it.

Obviously it would be yes as per me, being selfish is somewhere good rather it is better for us. If we talk about humans each one his or her life come to different situation and different circumstances that each one needs to face and come through it but it can't be that always you will win that situation that you met or you come through in your life more likely the changes are of loosing. one thing I would like to point out here that is the way we tackle that probllem it doesnt matters then if we fail that condition or come up with excellent results but if we are on positive way changes are there that we will get positive situations in our lives . In human being 's life there are three stages of our life that are childhood, youngage and oldage .so when we are at the very first stage of our life that is youngage that time we are very eager to learn many things which even we are unaware with but as we grow up we come to young age that is the stage of life where become mature and we start to sustain with society in a proper way.

In our youngage we try to do different type of experiment but ultimately we are unable to do with it as that time we are not with that much of capabilities that we can do certain thing in certain way as per wish and our desire as if it is childhood desires of a person can vary from person to person . always it wont be possible that whatever we are coming up with that will be happening the best one but trying for best is in our hand .

Then it comes to second stage of our life that is youngage it is the stage of our life where we start to have our opnion about certain things which wanted that things must happen in our life we give our best for that thing but sometimes we cant achieve it that time as per the particular person results would be one can be sad in hat situation, one can start to have some kind of excuses about himself, one can be the person to blame god else his destiny.

Here it comes to last stage of persons life that is old age even if we desire to do something new that time we are not able to do.

II
Content

"Everybody fails sometimes." "Failure makes you stronger." "Failure is the key to success." "who has never failed it means he never learned anything new". I'm sure we've all heard these sayings at one point in life or another.

We live in a society where all our achievements are appriciated on scales that have been devised. We have academic grades and degrees to measure how much we know, understand and remember; sports medals to show how much better we are at physical coordination than others and world records to show that we are literally the best in the whole world at a skill. Even abstract things like literature and art are compared and given awards. Failure is what happens when we can't prove that we're the best in the field that we have chosen.

failure= lack of success

Since childhood, we are pitted against one another. We've been told that to be the best is the only thing worth being. It is the only thing that will earn us respect from friends and make our parents proud. No wonder so many of us shudder at the thought of failure. We've learnt how to welcome and embrace success, but we haven't understood how to cope with failure.

We often look at great people—scientists, entrepreneurs, writers, artists and world leaders in respect. We're blinded by their achievements. We think that they're lucky that they've been given gifts that enable them to be the best. What we don't see is the most important aspect of their personalities—perseverance and constant improvement. There is not a single 'great man' out there who has not worked hard despite failing multiple times. What sets great people apart from other people is their attitude towards failure.

"I have not failed. I've just found 10,000 ways that won't work", said Thomas Edison, the inventor of the first incandescent light bulb.

Edison and his colleagues tested over 3,000 designs for the light bulb over a span of more than two years before finally arriving at an optimum design. He spent years learning from what didn't work and perfecting the design. Had he given up at the 2999th attempt, we wouldn't have had the design that led to the advanced lighting technology of today.

"If you fail, never give up because F.A.I.L. means 'First Attempt In Learning'", said Bharat Ratna
Dr. APJ Abdul Kalam, our nation's Missile Man and eleventh President.

During his career, Mr. Kalam encountered many failures—the premature death of the hovercraft project Nandi, the abandoning of RATO and ultimately, the failed launch of his SLV3 satellite, which happened while the entire nation was watching. Instead of giving up, he learnt from his mistakes and successfully launched the Rohini satellite into orbit less than a year later.

All these people tried and tried again until they succeeded. As all of these great personalities say, there is much to learn from failure. In the words of Albert Einstein, "Failure is success in progress". Failure shows us what we should not do. By critically analysing all the decisions taken before the failure, we can avoid it in the future. With an unbiased mind, we must survey our situation and find out what led to the failure. It is in this analysis that we can strengthen ourselves and our belief in the idea.

There are millions of ways to fail at something and only a few ways to succeed. Once we have tried and failed millions of times, we are bound to be successful. It is only a matter of patience and perseverance.

All of these instances display the indomitable spirit of people who have excelled in their field. We see that by constantly improving our idea, we can succeed. But besides perseverance, there is another aspect to success.

Failure does not mean that our ideas are not good. Sometimes, when the idea is novel, society may have a difficult time accepting it. Sometimes, we just need one more chance to prove that our idea will work. We don't always have to modify our ideas. Sometimes, they are already perfect.

"The difference in winning and losing is most often not quitting.",said Walt Disney, the creator of Disneyland which is reckoned by many as 'the Happiest Place on Earth.'

After a failed cartoon business and an unsuccessful career in acting, Disney had a copyright on a character he created taken away from him. In the midst of heavy debt, he introduced a new character 'Mickey Mouse'. Even after this being a success, no one was willing to take a risk on him. He was rejected over 300 times before one banker said yes to financially backing him. Instead of giving up in the face of adversity, he continued to believe in his ability and went on to create so many of the wonderful Disney characters we all know.

"Failure taught me things about myself that I could have learned no other way", says JK Rowling, the author of the bestselling series Harry Potter.

She was rejected by no less than twelve major publishers after finishing her first book. At the time, she was unemployed and was struggling to make ends meet. She would not be where she is today if she had not approached that thirteenth publisher. She shows us that what we need to believe in most, is ourselves.

Being rejected even though we know that our idea is good should strengthen our resolve to carry it out even more. The rejection teaches us that even if a small section of people do not accept the idea, it doesn't mean that the idea is not good. If our ideas are worth it, we must have unwavering belief in them.

Sometimes, other people can fail to recognise potential and may reject an unconventional idea. But we mustn't give up our individuality to conform to certain standards. Sometimes what other people see as an unfavourable trait can actually be advantageous.

We will be knowing about this in detail in this book about great people even they failed several times still they didnt gave up tried hard even very hard for there work because they knew one day will be there that will be the golden sunrise when the true determination will bring fruits to the way of consistency. many more we will understand about this in this book even some measures to be taken to reduce stress due to fear of failure.

Especially this book will guide childrens for motivating them and inspiring them in very interesting way.so lets have to ride to beautifull world of dreams and some attempts where one fails even though we know sometime that we have limited changes for doing this or that thing still some dont pay focus on that work.

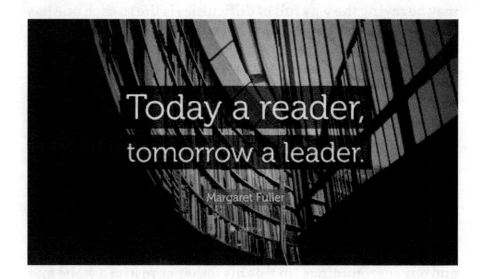

III

Life

Life

Like it is probably easy for each one to define life , some of you may say that life the journey from birth to death while others may be saying the way full of difficulties is life so each one has different way to view life. It is not even so easy for each one to live life rather I would say that living life is not easy task for anyone that is the reason why some stupid people give up as no longer they can sustain in this world . but as we all know there is something called god . then what is god? Answering to this question is very tedious task and its out of the box to answer this question .

As per many people the god is super power that is around us in this case too the answer will change from one person to other person. there was a boy he asked to his father that what is life and how are life can be different depending upon situation and our surroundings . to this his father gave him a stone and said to him go to market and sell this stone as he goes to market a lady asks him what is the cost of this stone , that time he remembers that his father told him if anyone asks you what is the cost of this stone just show your two fingers , he does it he shows his two fingers to the lady and then lady says it is for two rupee then he takes that two rupee comes to his father and then again his father gives him same kind of stone and tells him to go on stone shop then he goes there , the shopkeeper asks him what is the cost of the stone to this he shows his two fingers then the shopkeeper gives him 200 rupee after that he was amazed he comes back to his father and narrates whole story again his father gives him the same stone and tells him to on the jewellery shop and do the same as he goes on the jewellery shop and does the same thing of showing two finger when the shopkeeper asked him he was thrilled that time as the man gave him 2000 rupee. From this story we come to know that "WHERE WE PUT OUR LIFE ON THAT OUR LIFE CHANGES ".

Life teaches u

Here i would like to tell a story . there was girl how has failed in here exams , she was very upset and hurted , her father noticed that and then he called her in kitchen . then the girl went with her father in kitchen . her father put three bowls on stove of same size and he put equal amount of water in that bowls , then he took few potatoes, eggs and coffee beans and then he put potatoes in one bowl, eggs in other bowl and coffee beans in third bowl , then he on the stove that time after 15 mins he off the stove and then he took out potatoes, eggs and then with tea strainer he strain the coffee beans with water . Girl was not understanding anything. Then her father told to touch each item with hand then potatoes were soft , egg will more strong as compare to before boiling it and coffee beans were strain . so from this we understand that whenever the problems come to us we have to decide that we have to decide that like whom we should be like potatoes that before problem in life we are strong and after the problem we start to feel weak from inside, like egg that after problem we start being more strong or like coffee beans we will start to feel strong as well we will change our life.

You can change yourself and your life

When I was in grade4 I remember I use to read sometimes newspaper that time I read there I use to come to the syntax there everyday about government , today government made this changes that changes , everyone need to follow that ,I use to come to it and once I asked my father that who is this government I also want to be a government and I also want to rule country I thought it something that government is a person and makes some changes in our life and our world .

I once went to a library and there were many books once shelf was with life books , in that there was one book in which it was written that read this book it will change your like I thought that really lets try it then I took that book and I started to read it , once upon a time the god was living with humans , that time humans complained to god some farmers said that when we want rain it doesn't comes and then the person who wants to wash his clothes he says that when I want to wash my clothes there it rains . Once a farmer was highly unsatisfied with god rules and management he said god you are not doing good management that time good gives him all powers to make all the management whatever he wants then the farmer to his crops he gave fertile land proper sunlight, rain and eventually proper environment for growth of plant then he saw his good crops he went to god and he said that god see how I grown the crops that time god said check once by taking out chaff from it there were no wheat and some wheat haven't grown properly , so that time farmer asked god that was there any trick behind this , so the god said no . then farmer asked why did this happen then so then god relied that there was no struggle of seed in whole process and the take home of story was we must know our potential ,our weakness and with failures we must rise on too, because life is full of struggle and once you start to struggle the life ultimately gives fruits of your struggle.

The meaning of life, or the answer to the question: "What is the meaning of life?", pertains to the significance of living or existence in general. Many other related questions include: "Why are we here?", "What is life all about?", or "What is the purpose of existence?" There have been many proposed answers to these questions from many different cultural and ideological backgrounds. The search for life's meaning has produced much philosophical, scientific, theological, and metaphysical speculation throughout history. Different people and cultures believe different things for the answer to this question.

The meaning of life can be derived from philosophical and religious contemplation of, and scientific inquiries about existence, social ties, consciousness, and happiness. Many other issues are also involved, such as symbolic meaning, ontology, value, purpose, ethics, good and evil, free will, the existence of one or multiple gods, conceptions of God, the soul, and the afterlife. Scientific contributions focus primarily on describing related empirical facts about the universe, exploring the context and parameters concerning the "how" of life. Science also studies and can provide recommendations for the pursuit of well-being and a related conception of morality. An alternative, humanistic approach poses the question, "What is the meaning of my life?"

Researchers in positive psychology study empirical factors that lead to life satisfaction,full engagement in activities, making a fuller contribution by utilizing one's personal strengths,and meaning based on investing in something larger than the self. Large-data studies of flow experiences have consistently suggested that humans experience meaning and fulfillment when mastering challenging tasks and that the experience comes from the way tasks are approached and performed rather than the particular choice of task. For example, flow experiences can be obtained by prisoners in concentration camps with minimal facilities, and occur only slightly more often in billionaires. A classic example is of two workers on an apparently boring production line in a factory. One treats the work as a tedious chore while the other turns it into a game to see how fast she can make each unit and achieves flow in the process.

Neuroscience describes reward, pleasure, and motivation in terms of neurotransmitter activity, especially in the limbic system and the ventral tegmental area in particular. If one believes that the meaning of life is to maximize pleasure and to ease general life, then this allows normative predictions about how to act to achieve this. Likewise, some ethical naturalists advocate a science of morality—the empirical pursuit of flourishing for all conscious creatures.

Experimental philosophy and neuroethics research collects data about human ethical decisions in controlled scenarios such as trolley problems. It has shown that many types of ethical judgment are universal across cultures, suggesting that they may be innate, whilst others are culture-specific. The findings show actual human ethical reasoning to be at odds with most philosophical theories, for example consistently showing distinctions between action by cause and action by omission which would be absent from utility-based theories. Cognitive science has theorized about differences between conservative and liberal ethics and how they may be based on different metaphors from family life such as strong fathers vs nurturing mother models.

Neurotheology is a controversial field which tries to find neural correlates and mechanisms of religious experience. Some researchers have suggested that the human brain has innate mechanisms for such experiences and that living without using them for their evolved purposes may be a cause of imbalance. Studies have reported conflicting results on correlating happiness with religious belief and it is difficult to find unbiased meta-analyses.

Sociology examines value at a social level using theoretical constructs such as value theory, norms, anomie, etc. One value system suggested by social psychologists, broadly called Terror Management Theory, states that human meaning is derived from a fundamental fear of death, and values are selected when they allow us to escape the mental reminder of death.

Alongside this, there are a number of theories about the way in which humans evaluate the positive and negative aspects of their existence and thus the value and meaning they place on their lives. For example, depressive realism posits an exaggerated positivity in all except those experiencing depressive disorders who see life as it truly is, and David Benatar theorises that more weight is generally given to positive experiences, providing bias towards an over-optimistic view of life.

Emerging research shows that meaning in life predicts better physical health outcomes. Greater meaning has been associated with a reduced risk of Alzheimer's disease,reduced risk of heart attack among individuals with coronary heart disease, reduced risk of stroke.

Life refers to an aspect of existence. This aspect processes acts, evaluates, and evolves through growth. Life is what distinguishes humans from inorganic matter. Some individuals certainly enjoy free will in Life. Others like slaves and prisoners don't have that privilege. However, Life isn't just about living independently in society. It is certainly much more than that. Hence, quality of Life carries huge importance. Above all, the ultimate purpose should be to live a meaningful life. A meaningful life is one which allows us to connect with our deeper self.

One important aspect of Life is that it keeps going forward. This means nothing is permanent. Hence, there should be a reason to stay in dejection. A happy occasion will come to pass, just like a sad one. Above all, one must be optimistic no matter how bad things get. This is because nothing will stay forever. Every situation, occasion, and event shall pass. This is certainly a beauty of Life.

Many people become very sad because of failures. However, these people certainly fail to see the bright side. The bright side is that there is a reason for every failure. Therefore, every failure teaches us a valuable lesson. This means every failure builds experience. This experience is what improves the skills and efficiency of humans.

Probably a huge number of individuals complain that Life is a pain. Many people believe that the word pain is a synonym for Life. However, it is pain that makes us stronger. Pain is certainly an excellent way of increasing mental resilience. Above all, pain enriches the mind.

The uncertainty of death is what makes life so precious. No one knows the hour of one's death. This probably is the most important reason to live life to the fullest. Staying in depression or being a workaholic is an utter wastage of Life. One must certainly enjoy the beautiful blessings of Life before death overtakes.

Most noteworthy, optimism is the ultimate way of enriching life. Optimism increases job performance, self-confidence, creativity, and skills. An optimistic person certainly can overcome huge hurdles.

Meditation is another useful way of improving Life quality. Meditation probably allows a person to dwell upon his past. This way one can avoid past mistakes. It also gives peace of mind to an individual. Furthermore, meditation reduces stress and tension.

Pursuing a hobby is a perfect way to bring meaning to life. Without a passion or interest, an individual's life would probably be dull. Following a hobby certainly brings new energy to life. It provides new hope to live and experience Life.

In conclusion, Life is not something that one should take for granted. It's certainly a shame to see individuals waste away their lives. We should be very thankful for experiencing our lives. Above all, everyone should try to make their life more meaningful.

Life is a characteristic that distinguishes physical entities that have biological processes, such as signaling and self-sustaining processes, from those that do not, either because such functions have ceased (they have died), or because they never had such functions and are classified as inanimate. Various forms of life exist, such as plants, animals, fungi, protists, archaea, and bacteria. Biology is the science concerned with the study of life. There is currently no consensus regarding the definition of life. One popular definition is that organisms are open systems that maintain homeostasis, are composed of cells, have a life cycle, undergo metabolism, can grow, adapt to their environment, respond to stimuli, reproduce and evolve. Other definitions sometimes include non-cellular life such viruses and viroids. Abiogenesis is the natural process of life arising from non-living matter, such as simple organic compounds. The prevailing scientific hypothesis is that the transition from non-living to living entities was not a single event, but a gradual process of increasing complexity. Life on Earth first appeared as early as 4.28 billion years ago, soon after ocean formation 4.41 billion years ago, and not long after the formation of the Earth 4.54 billion years ago. The earliest known life forms are microfossils of bacteria. Researchers generally think that current life on Earth descends from an RNA world, although RNA-based life may not have been the first life to have existed. The classic 1952 Miller–Urey experiment and similar research demonstrated that most amino acids, the chemical constituents of the proteins us

in all living organisms, can be synthesized from inorganic compounds under conditions intended to replicate those of the early Earth. Complex organic molecules occur in the Solar System and in interstellar space, and these molecules may have provided starting material for the development of life on Earth.Since its primordial beginnings, life on Earth has changed its environment on a geologic time scale, but it has also adapted to survive in most ecosystems and conditions. Some microorganisms, called extremophiles, thrive in physically or geochemically extreme environments that are detrimental to most other life on Earth. The cell is considered the structural and functional unit of life. There are two kinds of cells, prokaryotic and eukaryotic, both of which consist of cytoplasm enclosed within a membrane and contain many biomolecules such as proteins and nucleic acids. Cells reproduce through a process of cell division, in which the parent cell divides into two or more daughter cells. In the past, there have been many attempts to define what is meant by "life" through obsolete concepts such as odic force, hylomorphism, spontaneous generation and vitalism, that have now been disproved by biological discoveries. Aristotle was the first person to classify organisms. Later, Carl Linnaeus introduced his system of binomial nomenclature for the classification of species. Eventually new groups and categories of life were discovered, such as cells and microorganisms, forcing dramatic revisions of the structure of relationships between living organisms. Though currently only known on Earth, life need not be restricted to it, and many scientists speculate in the existence of extraterrestrial life. Artificial life is a computer simulation or human-made reconstruction of any aspect of life, which is often used to examine systems related to natural life. Death is the permanent termination of all biological functions which sustain an organism, and as such, is the end of its life. Extinction is the term describing the dying out of a group or taxon, usually a species. Fossils are the preserved remains or traces of organisms.

The question of the meaning of life is perhaps one that we would rather not ask, for fear of the answer or lack thereof.

Still today, many people believe that we, humankind, are the creation of a supernatural entity called God, that God had an intelligent purpose in creating us, and that this intelligent purpose is "the meaning of life".

I do not propose to rehearse the well-worn arguments for and against the existence of God, and still less to take a side. But even if God exists, and even if He had an intelligent purpose in creating us, no one really knows what this purpose might be, or that it is especially meaningful.

The Second Law of Thermodynamics states that the entropy of a closed system—including the universe itself—increases up to the point at which equilibrium is reached, and God's purpose in creating us, and, indeed, all of nature, might have been no more lofty than to catalyse this process much as soil organisms catalyse the decomposition of organic matter.

If our God-given purpose is to act as super-efficient heat dissipators, then having no purpose at all is better than having this sort of purpose—because it frees us to be the authors of our purpose or purposes and so to lead truly dignified and meaningful lives.

In fact, following this logic, having no purpose at all is better than having any kind of pre-determined purpose, even more traditional, uplifting ones such as serving God or improving our karma.

In short, even if God exists, and even if He had an intelligent purpose in creating us (and why should He have had?), we do not know what this purpose might be, and, whatever it might be, we would rather be able to do without it, or at least to ignore or discount it. For unless we can be free to become the authors of our own purpose or purposes, our lives may have, at worst, no purpose at all, and, at best, only some unfathomable and potentially trivial purpose that is not of our own choosing.

You or others might object that not to have a pre-determined purpose is, really, not to have any purpose at all. But this is to believe that for something to have a purpose, it must have been created with that particular purpose in mind, and, moreover, must still be serving that same original purpose

Life in the concentration camp taught Frankl that our main drive or motivation in life is neither pleasure, as Freud had believed, nor power, as Adler had believed, but meaning. After his release, Frankl founded the school of logotherapy (from the Greek logos, meaning "reason" or "principle"), which is sometimes referred to as the "Third Viennese School of Psychotherapy" for coming after those of Freud and Adler. The aim of logotherapy is to carry out an existential analysis of the person, and, in so doing, to help her uncover or discover meaning for her life.

According to Frankl, meaning can be found through:

Experiencing reality by interacting authentically with the environment and with others.

Giving something back to the world through creativity and self-expression, and,

Changing our attitude when faced with a situation or circumstance that we cannot change.

"The point," said Frankl, "'is not what we expect from life, but rather what life expects from us."

We are constantly asked and/or asking what the meaning of life is. Truly, the answer will vary from person to person, it all depends on whom you are directing the question to. One might say that the meaning of life is money, for it is without it that we cannot survive. Another might say that it is friends or family, that very bond that we enjoy is the meaning of life. And another individual might say that it's love that is the meaning of life.In reality, no one really knows and there really isn't a direct answer to the question. To me, however, the meaning of life is about being who you are and being that well. Living each day truly well and being grateful for being on this side of the grass; never taking any day or anything nor anyone for granted. My Catholic School background taught me that and those quotes are taken from Saint Francis de Sales. Even if you are not a Catholic or a Christian for that matter, those quotes can still be put into practice by you regardless of your creed.

Being who you are and being that well is all about putting your talents to use and never taking them for granted. Realizing that you are unique and put here for a purpose. Everyone has talents and gifts, but not everyone uses them. I know at times I don't use my talents to their ability, but I'm trying. Some people's talents are those of great measure, some talents are little things that aren't always recognized, whatever the case may be, put them to good use. They might come in handy someday.

Living each day well can be a difficult task for the simple reason that life isn't always as predictable as we want it to be. Things happen, moods change, but the most important thing to realize is that we must appreciate the little things in life. The little things like where we are at this very moment while we're reading this article; the little things like who is important in your life. If someone is important or you love them, tell them. You might never get the chance to do it again. Tomorrow is promised to no man.

Finally, Carpe Diem. Seize the day. That is what life's all about. Seeing an opportunity and going after it knowing damn well that you have a chance to fail. Dare to fail and truly, nothing can go wrong.

All living organisms born and they die . the way between birth and death is our life that we live actually . if you have marked in birth certificate the date of birth is written on left side while on death certificate the date of deat is written on right side so the way between this two date we have to surpass that. humans have did the discoveries of many things from bulb to electricity , from hydroelectricity to solar electricity, from refrigeratoe to invetor but one thing is still not discovered I think you got it that is nothing but the time which is passed . humans have discovered many things so they have discovered it because they knw that the time which they have passed is not going to come again so each and every second they spend they think on that and finally they have successed in their life and they made all discoveries for our better of today so isnt it now our duty to start doing some useful things not for our generation but for us . so it starts with today no tommorow no yestreday but today .

looking towards the example of benjamin franklin he is the one who discovered "static electricity" he use to sell books and he was having a stationary shop of books once a man came to his shop and he ask the cost of book to his reply the worker of benjamin was there he said it cost is 100 dollar, then the customer said can the amount be lessed or can you decrease a little . the worker said,"no sorry " then the customer started fighting for it he said call our owner so the worker called benjamin and then when benjamin came and when the customer asked him the price he said it costs 150 dollar to customers surprise he said your worker said it is for 100 dollar , then to benjamins reply he told him that yes he was it is for 100 dollar but you wasted my time and for my time you need to give 150 and if you now start arguing then you need to give 200 dollar then customer understood his mistake and he gave 150 dollar and he took leave from there. the discoverers knew it that there time is going to finish and they knew it at any moment they can die so every moment they live like end minute of their life and each and every moment they utilise. time will never stop and you need to go on like time. we must think each and every moment like end moment as at really last moment we think all mistakes we commeted in our whole we always think about our past because after death our whole life will be like history like past . now stop crying because life will also cry when you will die so it is better to be happy in life to make us more happy at every moment we live . make your life happy and try to make others happy . you know that one day you are going to die one day , yes you know that . death is not happier ting and people feel it as bad when we talk about death people say talk about talk about something else ,but death is reality , but there are thousand of people who die and yes one day everything will be over .

so live a happy life

what is one thing that both rich and poor people can buy? yes thats happiness . happiness depends upon you your happiness i in your hand that you need to be happy or sad. everything happens for a reson in our life , each and everything . our life is just like a movie you will not understand that what you are doing now is for what let the climax come to your life you will understand that why this happened with you and what was the purpose behind it. keep trust on god , it doesnt matters you keep faith in you or not but start having faith on god and good deads.

stop comparing yourself with others stop having jelousness about other stop comparing if someone is more rich than you then the thing is you start being jealous about that person but if he is rich than it doesnt mean that he is more happier a car cant bring happiness in your life yes it can but for 1 or 2 months not for your whole life. love yourself , start loving yourself if you see others doing that you will do that but no what you are start rising in your field what you are in start progressing in that because what others do that doesnt mean to you behave like you are the one who can do it and you must also try for . because onece you start loving yourself and being best for you not for others you will be the happiest person in world so be change that you.

her is one story which I woul like to tell there was a boy who was hungry for success all that he waant was success everthing which meaned to him was success. once his running competition was there and he was preparing for that the next day two boys with him came for running with hi they ranned with him and they boy winned . all people around him cheered for him but their was a old man who didnt showed any sentiments then next two boys came and they ran with him he won again and again the crowd waved at the boy now still the old man didnt show any sentiments then th e boy said is there any one who can race with me the old man came forward and then with him he brought one old lady and a blind man they both were unable to walk and the boy said is it a race and then old man said you start running and then boy ran and he winned both the lady and man were at starting line but this time crowd didnt show any type of sentiment and then the boy was in thinking that now one is ready to be part of my success , then again the old man said to run with them now this time he walked so slowly with them and they crossed finishing line toogether this time the crowd was cheerig for them , the old man told him that in your life if you will win always, then who was challenger for you in your life and with whom were you fighting .

"Life is not about the door that will open or the door that closed. It is about enjoying the hell in the hallway."

In taking the next small step, always remember that it might be the wrong step. That's ok. The important part of any step is the insight that follows. Not the result, but the lesson. In school, they call learning "lessons." Learning is the lesson.

Life is about learning.

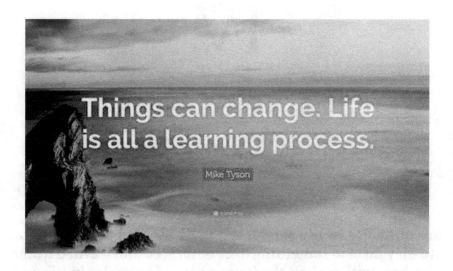

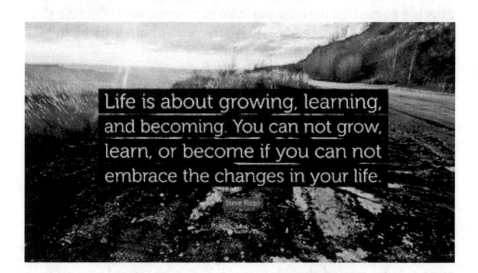

IV

Obstacles in life

Are obstacles in life something to be avoided at all costs, or are they instead something to be embraced and learned from? This post will explore the importance of obstacles in life and discuss why it's essential to face them head-on. We'll also provide some tips on how you can overcome any obstacle that comes your way. So, read on to learn more about why obstacles are essential in life!

Obstacles help us grow and learn new things. Without them, we would never reach our full potential. So why are obstacles important in life? Because they teach us how to overcome adversity and become better people. When you think about it, life is one big obstacle course. You're constantly meeting new challenges and trying to overcome them. At first glance, this might seem like a bad thing. Why can't life be easy? But if you look a little closer, you'll see that obstacles are a good thing. When we're faced with a challenge, we have two choices: We can back down and shrink from it, or we can stand up and face it head-on. Which is going to make you a better person? The answer is obvious: It's the second option. By learning how to overcome obstacles, we become stronger as individuals.

Obstacles help us grow

Every time you meet an obstacle, you're forced to learn something new and adapt to your environment. You become a better person because of it. If life were always accessible, we would never grow as people. We'd stay stuck in the same old rut forever. And that's no fun at all!

Obstacles force us to adapt

If life were easy, you would never learn how to adapt and grow as a person. Without the challenge of obstacles, you wouldn't feel like you had to improve yourself because things will always be easier for you. But when faced with an obstacle, you have no choice but to adapt. And as a result, your sense of self-worth improves.

Obstacles deepen our understanding of life

We can learn a lot from obstacles, even if they directly affect us! When you look at something from a distance, it's easy to judge it and say, "I wouldn't do that." But once you're forced to face it head-on, things become a little different. For example, joining a Toastmasters club can be pretty scary if you're afraid of public speaking. But eventually, you might find that there's nothing to fear!

Obstacles help us learn from our mistakes

When you run into an obstacle, it's not because you're a bad person or anything like that. It's usually because you made a mistake somewhere along the line (at least, that's often the case). By learning from your mistakes and avoiding them in the future, life will be much easier for you.

Obstacles don't have to be a bad thing. On the contrary, they're essential in life because they force us to grow and improve as individuals. When you think about it that way, overcoming challenges is a good thing!

Everyone who wants success in life encounters obstacles along the way. However, successful people know how to overcome these obstacles and continue marching toward their goals, no matter what gets in their way. If you're having trouble achieving your professional or personal ambitions, it might be time to consider these common obstacles that professionals face.

Self-doubt

Everyone gets self-doubts now and then, but for professionals who are still climbing the ladder to success, it's an obstacle that must be overcome! When you have doubts about your abilities or qualifications, it becomes straightforward to become demotivated. The key is to stay motivated despite self-doubt.

Fear of failure

This hurdle is very familiar to most professionals at the beginning stages of their careers. The fear of failure is often paralyzing, and it stops people from taking risks that could be rewarding. If you're afraid of failing, you can either run away from your goals or learn to overcome that fear. The latter is the better option!

Loneliness

Success could indeed lead to money, power, and fame, but it can also leave you feeling very alone at times. Sometimes you have to move away from your family or friends to live up to your ambitions. If you're okay with that, then you can overcome loneliness.

1) Believe in yourself:

Believing in yourself and your abilities is key to overcoming obstacles. Without faith, it's hard to push ahead. When you believe in yourself, the world opens up before you and letting go of those obstacles becomes more accessible.

2) Allow other people to help you when needed:

You can rely on others to help you when needed. You don't always have to go it alone, and letting people in is essential for overcoming obstacles.

3) Do not give up under pressure:

It's easy to panic when faced with an obstacle and lose hope. But the best thing you can do is keep your cool and push ahead!

4) Stay calm and focused when things get tough:

When your plans are threatened, it's easy to lose focus. But if you can keep yourself clear and focused, you'll be able to overcome even the most challenging obstacles!

5) Learn from your mistakes:

By learning from your mistakes when you hit an obstacle, you'll gain the knowledge necessary to succeed in the future.

So next time you're met with an obstacle, remember that it's not a bad thing at all. Obstacles don't have to be something that holds us back; they can push us forward! With faith in yourself and the help of others around you, there's no limit to what you can achieve.

The critic inside you is probably the most powerful obstacle of all.

It makes you second-guess yourself. It demotivates you and crushes your desires. It's basically your super-ego reminding you to conform with the norms you've been taught by parents and society. The norms that keep 99% of people stuck in average lives.

You've got to tune out your internal critic. Because believe it or not, you won't be defeated by what others say about you...

Excuses

You need to forget about what you don't have or what you wish you had, and focus on what you've got. Because what you've got right now is a lot.The secret is to realize that you, and only you, are responsible for what you do with it.Successful people don't allow excuses to limit them. They take control of their situation and focus on solutions that move them forward.So you can let excuses kill your conscience or you can do something about it.

Complacency

Most people settle for mediocrity and accept it as a cultural norm. They live regrettable lives, work at jobs they hate, build their family on a foundation of debt, and then they die.That might seem depressing and hurtful, but life doesn't care about your feelings.You can't just sit back and be satisfied with the life you have right now. There's a lot more you can do and accomplish. You just have to want it as bad as you want to sleep or party.So you might as well raise your standards and get busy living.

fear

"Fear kills dreams. Fear kills hope. Fear put people in the hospital. Fear can age you. Fear can hold you back from doing something that you know within yourself that you are capable of doing, but it will paralyze you."
– Les Brown

You're always saying that you need to make more money, start a business, change your life, etc. But you don't do it. Why?Because you're afraid. You're afraid of failing and you're also afraid to succeed.In both cases the lack of knowledge causes these feelings, which makes you less confident in your abilities.However, you have access to that knowledge all around you. Resources like this site contain valuable content to guide you towards your goals. But it's up to you to seize it and use it to change your life.

social media and television

"Tv is so bad. It is a tool by the media to not make people think."
– Naveen Andrews

You don't need a research study to know how much of your life is consumed by digital media. You can validate it on your own just by observing yourself.Netflix marathons, reality tv, news, and social media, all consume a large part of your day. And despite these things doing nothing to enrich your life or get you closer to becoming wealthy, you still enjoy them.You somehow manage to do all those activities, yet when it comes to reading, getting healthy or working on your goals... you're always busy.It's tragic. But it also explains why poor people collect the latest consumer gadgets and rich people collect tons of books.

V

life is like game

Is life just a simple game for you? Do you level up? Do you get new skills and experiences that can help you win the game of life?

I love the concept of treating life as a game. I often think this to myself and see life as a game where you need to level up, continue to build and grow as a person. Think of monopoly... it's kind of like growing your assets, continually building and reaching another level.

Today, we have a guest post from Derek McCullough who explores this concept further to help you learn how you can start to live life like a game.

There are many levels we play as we grow up. We start at Level 1 not knowing how to walk or feed ourselves. Sooner or later we end up on Level 20, or Level 30. Whatever Level you want to call what you're on now.

We go through high school, we sometimes go to college, and we get jobs and pay bills. We find the routine, start to live it, and then never stop.

We can get stuck on this level. The going to work, coming home, doing nothing, and repeating level that we never seem to beat. We're going to work and doing what we're supposed to do, but our lives are moving at such a slow pace it doesn't even feel like we're alive anymore. Well, we're kinda not.

I'll admit that not long ago I had almost resigned to living that life. Playing out the same level. Grinding it out. Little by little, hand over hand, slowly making my way to the next level. At least I thought I'd make it to the next level.

Each level of life should be challenging to you, but not hard on you. Throughout your game of life, you should feel uncomfortable, but not be in pain, depressed, or unhappy. If you feel negative, you're stuck on a level you don't particularly like. You're stuck in a game you don't like.

Remember, you're the player. You're in control. You choose the game. You choose the rules. You can choose a different level.

In a video game, the character you play will have a set number of lives. They are a limited number of chances to succeed. This was usually the case back in the days of the arcade and still remains true in some games. In special cases and with certain "cheat" codes, you are able to unlock unlimited lives, meaning you have an unlimited numbers of opportunities to succeed.

Life is actually the same case. You have unlimited "lives". Until the figure in the black robe with the giant scythe comes and presses your power button, you can keep trying and trying to beat the level you're on. You can change the game and play out a different story.

You aren't stuck in any level or in any game. You're stuck because you're doing it the same way. You keep trying to tackle a problem with the same methods.

Look back at the challenges you've conquered. Identify what it is that made you succeed. Combine previous tactics and modify those strategies to attack your problems from a different angle, with added gusto.

Remember, as long as you keep playing the game, no matter if you "die" on a given attempt, you always have the chance to try again. Attack it a different way. Change it up, and you'll find the successful strategy. Then, learn and be better prepared for the next, tougher level.

Great games are fun, and so life should be. I'm sure you don't want to trudge and slog your way through an ordinary life, so don't. Choose a life full of adventure and challenges.

Maybe that means choosing a different game than the one your playing, the game you might feel stuck at. Whatever you end up choosing, you never fail if you don't give up. Quitting is true failure. Temporary failure is the learning required to finally beat the game. It's the key to finally winning.In the history of games, there have been games designed to teach people the hidden meaning of life, death and the afterlife, like Senet, an ancient Egyptian game where the movement of the pieces followed the soul's journey through the afterlife. In medieval India, a popular game was Gyan Chauper, in which players tried to move their pieces towards Moksha or ultimate liberation. Along the journey, the pieces could move up ladders - representing virtuous actions - or down snakes - representing vices. The soul could be one square away from liberation, only to tumble down a large snake - how often this seems to happen to spiritual gurus!

American Puritans developed a similar game in the 19th century called The Mansion of Happiness, in which players moved across squares representing the Christian virtues and vices until they reached heaven (shown on the left). However, in 1860 a new version of the game was developed, called The Chequered Game of Life, in which the object was not to get to heaven but rather to get rich, get a family, and retire in a nice home. That version - now called simply The Game of Life - is still played today. We edited heaven out of the game of life.

Today, we can create games that are so immersive, so huge, so brimming with intelligence, that we feel like we're in another world, a world of humans' own creation. That's what I felt when I played Grand Theft Auto for several days in a row - there were so many missions and side-missions, the world of the game was so changeable, so beautiful, so full of interesting characters, that I became totally absorbed in that world.

And when you can create games which are that absorbing and immersive, you can start to see this world as a game, a virtual reality. And that's precisely what's happened in the last few years - various philosophers and futurists have suggested we're actually living in a virtual simulation, created by future humans or some other intelligent species.

VI

Give your best

The ball is smacked over the net falling quickly to the shinny wood flooring. I dive to the ground, reach out an arm, letting the white ball hit against my pale arms turning them bright red. I push the ball over the net and get back up on my feet ready for the next ball that comes my way. I love playing sports, especially volleyball. The excitement in the games is overwhelming, and you have to be ready at all times for a ball to come flying your way. I always try to contribute to the team so I won't let my teammates down even if it means falling to the ground to get the ball. I believe that you should always try your best even when things are difficult.

Trying your best when things are difficult will not only make you a stronger player, but when you work hard and try your best it makes others respect for you grow. When you work hard others know that you care about what you are doing and that you are dedicated.

I have always admired Martin Luther King Jr's ability to work hard and try his best in difficult situations. His strong voice billows deep from within in him. He preaches words of encouragement, strength and dedication. His voice rings in peoples ears. You can tell by his face that he wants everyone one that listens to be inspired and that he is trying his very best to make people understand. Though Martin Luther King was discriminated against constantly he always tried his best to create equality for African Americans. He never gave up and always tried to help. Martin Luther King had one of the most difficult situations but he stilled tried to his best to make the world a better place. He lived through constant ridicule and harassment, but he always fought for what he believed in.

Trying your best is always a great way to encourage and motivate people but it is also very helpful to yourself. The night before a huge test, stressful and panic filled. How will I ever learn all of this? I scramble through all of my notes franticly, shuffling papers and reading and rereading definitions. I try my best to learn all the information, and by the end of the night, I thought I had got it down. It was worth the extra effort and hard work because the day I got my test back I was thrilled with my score. So even when it is difficult and you think to yourself that you can't do it, remember that you should always try you best even when things are difficult because it will pay off in the long run.

Even though you can never go back and change a time when you slacked off during practice or didn't study enough for a test, you should always try your best in the future even when things are difficult. As Eleanor Roosevelt once said, "You have to accept whatever comes and the only important thing is that you meet it with the best you have to give."

The ball is smacked over the net falling quickly to the shinny wood flooring. I dive to the ground, reach out an arm, letting the white ball hit against my pale arms turning them bright red. I push the ball over the net and get back up on my feet ready for the next ball that comes my way. I love playing

FAILURES ARE THE PILLARS TO SUCCESS

sports, especially volleyball. The excitement in the games is overwhelming, and you have to be ready at all times for a ball to come flying your way. I always try to contribute to the team so I won't let my teammates down even if it means falling to the ground to get the ball. I believe that you should always try your best even when things are difficult.

Trying your best when things are difficult will not only make you a stronger player, but when you work hard and try your best it makes others respect for you grow. When you work hard others know that you care about what you are doing and that you are dedicated.

I have always admired Martin Luther King Jr's ability to work hard and try his best in difficult situations. His strong voice billows deep from within in him. He preaches words of encouragement, strength and dedication. His voice rings in peoples ears. You can tell by his face that he wants everyone one that listens to be inspired and that he is trying his very best to make people understand. Though Martin Luther King was discriminated against constantly he always tried his best to create equality for African Americans. He never gave up and always tried to help. Martin Luther King had one of the most difficult situations but he stilled tried to his best to make the world a better place. He lived through constant ridicule and harassment, but he always fought for what he believed in.

Trying your best is always a great way to encourage and motivate people but it is also very helpful to yourself. The night before a huge test, stressful and panic filled. How will I ever learn all of this? I scramble through all of my notes franticly, shuffling papers and reading and rereading definitions. I try my best to learn all the information, and by the end of the night, I thought I had got it down. It was worth the extra effort and hard work because the day I got my test back I was thrilled with my score. So even when it is difficult and you think to yourself that you can't do it, remember that you should always try you best even when things are difficult because it will pay off in the long run.

Even though you can never go back and change a time when you slacked off during practice or didn't study enough for a test, you should always try your best in the future even when things are difficult. As Eleanor Roosevelt once said, "You have to accept whatever comes and the only important thing is that you meet it with the best you have to give."

We have all heard, "Always do your best." Whether it came from our parents, a teacher or sports coach, doing our best has always been a cliche-motto echoed throughout our lives. But what does doing your best really mean? And is it even possible to always do your best?

Emphatically I say yes, yes it is.

For years I believed that I was failing at everything I tried to do in life. I found that I allowed small let downs to snowball, steering my self esteem into nonexistence. Eventually I fully believed that I was worthless and had no potential.

One realization that I learned from depression was that I always put so much stress on myself which led to an intense shadow of dissatisfaction following me wherever I went. I would always second guess myself and no matter how hard I tried, felt like I was never doing well enough.

What does doing your best really mean?

Doing your best is synonymous with living out each and every moment to its fullest potential. And this potential exists in every situation you encounter in your life. All that is required of you is not to fight whatever life throws your way.

Doing your best is not about meeting expectations or achievements. It isn't about success or failure (or whatever that label even implies). It is about putting all your energy into whatever life situation you are currently experiencing.

We have all heard, "Always do your best." Whether it came from our parents, a teacher or sports coach, doing our best has always been a cliche-motto echoed throughout our lives. But what does doing your best really mean? And is it even possible to always do your best?

Emphatically I say yes, yes it is.

For years I believed that I was failing at everything I tried to do in life. I found that I allowed small let downs to snowball, steering my self esteem into nonexistence. Eventually I fully believed that I was worthless and had no potential.

One realization that I learned from depression was that I always put so much stress on myself which led to an intense shadow of dissatisfaction following me wherever I went. I would always second guess myself and no matter how hard I tried, felt like I was never doing well enough.

What does doing your best really mean?

Doing your best is synonymous with living out each and every moment to its fullest potential. And this potential exists in every situation you encounter in your life. All that is required of you is not to fight whatever life throws your way.

Doing your best is not about meeting expectations or achievements. It isn't about success or failure (or whatever that label even implies). It is about putting all your energy into whatever life situation you are currently experiencing.

For instance, if you are a baseball player and you constantly are thinking about doing your best, it is going to distract your attention away from hitting a fastball moving at ninety miles an hour. Similarly, if you're a scientist or philosopher, then thinking about doing your best will interfere with thinking about the task you're trying to solve at hand.

The point is, that you just have to live each and every moment with the intention of giving your all to the present, whatever that entails. You can't do your best if you are worried that you that you could be doing better. Otherwise you are no different than a dog chasing its tail!

Take any opportunity in life as a new adventure. Even if it is something that you have done a thousand times, experience it to its fullest from an open-minded perspective. For example, take your time spent waiting in line as an opportunity to talk to a stranger or appreciate the environment you're in rather than anxiously thinking about how miserable you are because everyone else is moving slowly.

Do things to do them, not get them done. There are a lot of situations in life that we dread. For example, if you have to clean something, the mind often immediately races to, "I can't wait until this is done." Instead of dreading something until its done, take it as an opportunity to fully invest yourself in. This might sound silly, but it is such a simple way to re-frame your mind that will make everything you do more enjoyable.Intentions are great, but they only get you so far. Have you ever heard of the phrase "fake it 'till you make it?" I believe that this phrase fundamentally means acting even if the motivation isn't there. Just because you think you can't do something doesn't mean you can't.

Investing all your energy into the moment and away from thinking about how the moment could be better is a practice that will improve all areas of your life.

If you always invest all your energy you have into conscious life and away from the unconscious mind then you will always be doing your best. Don't fear that you won't do as well as you want or you will succumb to those fears.

By staying in the moment and becoming fully present your mind begins to fear the future and harp on the past less and less. You become less dependent on external validation. You spend less time setting expectations and more time actually doing the things that will lead you towards achieving your goals.

When you always do your best you will be amazed by the results. It is a program for living that progresses the more you work it.If you're reading Forbes, you may already have embraced your own ambitious streak. No matter what you're trying to accomplish, with thousands of other people trying to do the same thing, it surely helps to be driven. After all, most of the greatest entrepreneurs, politicians, scientists, and artists were perpetually striving to beat their personal best or challenge the status quo. Yet being driven to succeed should not be confused with the kind of competitive ambition that can consume you. So, do you need to be competitive with others, and what is the essential difference between "being the best" and "doing your best"?

Ambition can be all about achieving success on your own terms, whereas competitiveness means striving to be more successful than others.

The key, says psychiatrist and author Dr. Neel Burton, is to pursue healthy ambition - not looking over your shoulder at how others are faring, but simply doing your best: "People with a high degree of healthy ambition are those with the insight and strength to control the blind forces of ambition, shaping [it] so that it matches their interests and ideals. They harness it so that it fires them without also burning them or those around them."

The main difference between my British and American clients is their attitude towards the whole spectrum of ambitious behavior. In the USA, "taking care of Number One" is not only accepted but encouraged, whereas in Britain all personal ambition has long been considered to be vulgar. In Britain, you can make your way right to the very top of the corporate or social ladder, just so long as no one sees you climbing.

A British executive interviewed by Sam Friedman and Daniel Laurison, in their devastating new book The Class Ceiling:

Why it Pays to be Privileged, describes the accepted code at work: "It was instantly recognizable to me, exactly like the common rooms at school and at Oxford. The rules are: it's good to be right, but it's better to be funny!"

However, whereas naked ambition is often encouraged in the USA, corporations on both sides of the Atlantic tend to avoid hiring people with a competitive streak. That's because being the best means putting yourself first. It is the opposite of being collaborative.

Have you got enough ambitious people around you?

Befriending and learning from role models and mentors who are smarter and more successful than you will help expand your sense of possibility. Even if you aren't competing with them, their energy will rub off on you. "Talk with and learn from people different from you," suggests strategy adviser Jason Ma, who refers to what he calls the Power of Proximity. "Be open to dialogue with acquaintances and even select strangers.

Are you willing to take risks?

Ambition takes a willingness to step into fear and anxiety, says psychiatrist Dr. Neel Burton, "Some people are better able to tolerate this fear, perhaps because they are more courageous, committed, or driven, and can minimize the fear," he says. "Ambitious people act with purpose, but allow themselves room to explore, experiment and discover."

Whenever you're next in doubt about whether you're being competitive or ambitious, ask yourself this: "Am I really trying to do my best or is this about my need to be the best?" Chances are, you'll be able to tell which state you're in just by how you feel in your body.

VII

Blossom in you

Everyone has different ambition, goal, dreams that each needs to Achieve in his or her life. As the person of beautiful planet earth need to do some or any other thing which is good, or it can be even best but it must not be bad or worst. As each one of us come through to many pathways in his life that always clear that your dreams always they won't be full filled by you because it is not possible for one to do for it. Most important thing in our lives is to be happy and make others happy because there is only thing by which people will remember you in his or her life that is to make that person Happy because l don't think there may be a person who don't like happiness in his life. Everyone wanted to be happy and joyful, but everyone can't get it.

One thing which is surely to be determined is that we all must be consistent, focused and ambitious. Most important for each one is to be humble and patient as this two these things are only there which will keep person's heart, mind and soul happy and excited. More even one should learn to do some creative things which are to be deserved by a one. Always learn to be like a leaf some or other day you need to fall. Always everyone experiences certain things and learns from it some or other thing. So experiences teaches us more than anything. Each thing matters to you when you matter to that thing so always keep in mind that if you will be just a piece of any war or any situation you can change the whole scenario that power you have. So don't judge your self in any circumstances. Everyone in his life fail once some of them after failure have a spirit to rise up but some people once they fail they think that they are the failures of whole life they never try to succeed in their life. But actually failures are there pillars to success. Success is essential in each once life but with that each needs to do handwork , smart work and consistency is vital. Learn to do time management because once the time has passed it will not come back so each minute you waste will not come back keep this in mind before you waste it every minute is important and precious in your life a minute can change your dreams aaand life too so have that capacity to sustain the capacity you waste time and don't call the time passed as time pass do something good even if it's not related to study do some or any other thing creative. One day will be there in your life that time you will be happy for yourself but for what you have done in the way if you do good things result will be also good but if you do bad things result will be also bad . So which results you want depends on your karma that you do on your deeds you do so the path of life depends upon you that you want to choose. Always in your life you will not shine rather you would only shine if you keep your self unlimited don't keep your self limited. If you limit yourself then you can't shine one day of your life to be the to have spirit shine more and more and don't let the dust cover dust means the negativity in your mind clean that and happy and keep in your control don't let it divert from your dreams and goals be positive and bring positivity in you. Everyone has certain problem but there is always a solution for each of them solution comes to you when you try hard for it.Solutions don't come automatically you need to work for it.

Sometimes question mark Comes to you when you are with confusions Certain times in your life question mark comes what to do and what to not am I going right or wrong on the path of your life or on each one's have to go for such situations but you need to go beyond that question mark and solve it . Most probably this question mark comes to the children's are the students while solving the paper like if a concept is not understood by any of children teachers asks them why there is question mark on your face.

Somewhere the ladders of right path take you right destination just you need to follow that and ultimate the result you will get will be more better than your works you did always remember one time the steps you work on right path will always give you back the right results you want so before walking and selecting the path you wanted remember that results you are going to get will depend upon your deeds independent upon that take your steps be careful. Sometimes in your life life will punch you just to check that house strong you are it's not probable that each one is with many punch but certainly in many of the cases each one has one has to face. Most important thing to succeed in life is have you behave with your life are you cheating yourself or your parents or your dreams that you need to decide before you cheat. So how you be have you behave and have you are with the people depends more than have you are acting to them have your showing yourself to them have you representing you in front of all. Ultimately the three keys that you need to follow to show yourself a genuine person is to be humble, patient and consistent with work.

This is the real fact of our life that life is just like a game sometimes you lose and other time you win but always it will not be that you will just been or you will just leave that would be a day that you will lose and that would be a day that you will win but one thing that can happen continuously is working hard showing your determination towards that particular task . Show that you are better than anyone.

Most important thing is very keep your life to keep your life in a certain situations in a certain area where you are going to get sudden stress and just confusions so you will definitely fill sad always and always disheartened at the way you leave the way you keep your life in a certain situations will depend will depend definitely as you need to show and you need to work on it before you show it. Some way you will feel that I am not down somewhere you will feel that I need to give up on so that time just have patience and rest take a break and start again at the break you take should not be a break for your whole life take a small break to feel you relaxed and refresh again have some vacations . Something more enjoyable to get relax from your daily routines and schedule to make yourself again energetic and enthusiastic.

Sometimes it will happen that something will happen which you haven't hope for any time in your life but you need to go from that and you need to finish that you will start to fill surprised and confused and what is happening with me so that time only one Mantra can help you and that's nothing but to be come to be patient and see what happens this you have to be strong every circumstances of your life ultimately the results will succeed you and your life and in your dreams.

Most important thing in your life is that you should have ambition you should have a dream you should have a goal because the life is just useless if you don't have any one of it if you are not having this things your life then why you are leaving for what's the use of your life. If you are born when is your duty if your job before becoming any of the person that you have to be a person will make others happy not be the reason for other sadness.

Dreams come true when you try hard for it. Even it is said by a great person which you probably know that is APJ Abdul Kalam the dreams are not those that you seen your sleep but dreams are those that don't let you sleep. So which dreams you need to have you need to decide that because always it will be the not case that you will have peaceful sleep.

Even your friends play a key roll in your life inshaping your life and your history as the friends you make will make your day will make your month and whole year. Your companions will play a vital role in your behaviour in your daily schedule are the only once go to whom you will come across certain difficulties and happiness to but it depends on your friends that have they are So make good friends and being good companions.

To be a good person you should show a helping hand to others. You should show respect and self dignity to yourself to actually being helpful sometime good and few times bad to because certain situations and that time you don't have to help others like while exams if you tell answers to your friends that is not a help actually your wasting your friends life summer otherwise if we check on.

Most important thing is to show brotherhood learn to make more people and to join people with you be the one to love people and make relationships with not to destroy the relationship because most important thing in today's world is not money is to have people with you and humanities because humans need humidity. No use of human without humanity. You need to show your talent and skills but in front of all because as you don't show your talent and skills and front of all then what's the use of which you are not showing in front of all that this kills the talent you have some peoples are there who can't express that their skills and their talent is there if you show that you would be a rockstar.

Most important thing again is confidence you have because if you are excellent in all the things it means that you are all rounder and multi talented but if you have confidence you then you can't fall in any way if you have confidence if you have that self belief that you are going to do it so you will but if you don't have that confidence the certain type of self belief in yourself and whatever may happen if you are not confident then definitely it can't be confident about yourself and your dreams too. You can show to all that how you can fly very far and very high if you have certain type of skills in you fly high you need is your spirit and focus to your goals and your dreams just you need to do is you have to work with expecting no results you have to work hard then you expected in certain cases it happens with many of the peoples that they expect other would be the best and unfortunately than no more better to so you have to give your best and expect little.

You need to show that kind of self respect to others that kind of dignity to others that kind of things you would get back . To Achieve each of that you need to be the one to spark and show your talent infront of all show your talent your skills to all be the one to shine more and more than ever.be the one to be more unique and more life longing person show your fluttering wings to all .

At the birth of each human being each one is just like a diamond but as you start to grow on your dead what you perform from that diamond you become gold from gold silver and from silver to bronze ultimately no more you are any of those just you are now a coal it happens because of your deeds no one from the born to the death remains a diamond if he remains then he is real person he is real diamond .

Doors of opportunities are open for you just you need to enter it. Ultimately the doors are open throughout your life just a thing is you don't see those and if you see them still you are in confusions that to enter it or not Opportunities don't come you need to create them so creating them is with you and you can do it for sure so create it if you can't see any . This world is full of magics and wonderful and exciting things but more exciting you can create to show all that you are also a magician who can create magics which are even more fantabulous . This world is just a image infront of you if you don't enter in it if you don't show your character in it if you don't play any character in it so you need to be more than ever and be the one who is center of attraction in whole scenario and image which will look more and far better due to you so it must look realistic and more wonderful.

Never give up on your dreams because one day you will be the winner and you don't know that when you will be winner . Never give up in any competition in any race because life is itself a biggest race which even more biggest dress in year journey because in this place if you win that means that you have been whole resem your life it will come with different and different types of hurdles with you need to cross .Never give up on your dreams because one day you will be the winner and you don't know that when you will be winner . Never give up in any competition in any race because life is itself a biggest race which even more biggest dress in year journey because in this place if you win that means that you have been whole resem your life it will come with different and different types of hurdles with you need to cross .One day or any other day will be there when you will fly just like a rocket in the sky if you want to fly just like rocket you need to boost up like it and you will see whole world in space. It will seem to you a wonderful mass piece just like you don't judge yourself that you can't be a one you can be a one to change the whole world even whole space to.One day or any other day will be there when you will fly just like a rocket in the sky if you want to fly just like rocket you need to boost up like it and you will see whole world in space. It will seem to you a wonderful mass piece just like you don't judge yourself that you can't be a one you can be a one to change the whole world even whole space to.

Never you are less than anyone all are same all are God gifted just the thing is have you behave and your manner towards your life you choose to flyover to have the flight just light and flight in your life. Rockets are there many aeroplanes are there but you know one day you can take place of that flight going high and high where your news will be spread all to the peoples of the country of the world's and of the spaceNever you are less than anyone all are same all are God gifted just the thing is have you behave and your manner towards your life you choose to flyover to have the flight just light and flight in your life. Rockets are there many aeroplanes are there but you know one day you can take place of that flight going high and high where your news will be spread all to the peoples of the country of the world's and of the space.

I think in each and everyone's life this situation is occurred that when from both side you are pulled on and you don't know that where to go on from this side or that side because like from both the side there some of the advantages and some of the disadvantages to so becomes little difficult for you from the which way you are going to go on and from which way you have to blossom to.I think in each and everyone's life this situation is occurred that when from both side you are pulled on and you don't know that where to go on from this side or that side because like from both the side there some of the advantages and some of the disadvantages to so becomes little difficult for you from the which way you are going to go on and from which way you have to blossom to.

I think in each and everyone's life this situation is occurred that when from both side you are pulled on and you don't know that where to go on from this side or that side because like from both the side there some of the advantages and some of the disadvantages to so becomes little difficult for you from the which way you are going to go on and from which way you have to blossom to.I think in each and everyone's life this situation is occurred that when from both side you are pulled on and you don't know that where to go on from this side or that side because like from both the side there some of the advantages and some of the disadvantages to so becomes little difficult for you from the which way you are going to go on and from which way you have to blossom to.

But ther is one person always behind us like for every successful person there is a person behind him and everything one of that because of home you are at right path and you are just rocking on. So the place where you have reached always remember one time in your life that due to home you are here due to who is efforts you have reached this place always have realisation of that thing.But ther is one person always behind us like for every successful person there is a person behind him and everything one of that because of home you are at right path and you are just rocking on. So the place where you have reached always remember one time in your life that due to home you are here due to who is efforts you have reached this place always have realisation of that thing.

You need to struggle for each thing in your life upto the time you are children you will get spoon feeding but as you will grow up then it will stop ultimately you need to work for it then stood up for it then as well as work for it then . This is going to happen definitely really it is truth and fact of each once life .You need to struggle for each thing in your life upto the time you are children you will get spoon feeding but as you will grow up then it will stop ultimately you need to work for it then stood up for it then as well as work for it then . This is going to happen definitely really it is truth and fact of each once life .

Try to be happier than you be sad learn to enjoy your life more than you struggle for it, be the one to tackle through difficulty and then what comes to you is the way you react to it . be happy more than you be sad and being overjoyed .Try to be happier than you be sad learn to enjoy your life more than you struggle for it, be the one to tackle through difficulty and then what comes to you is the way you react to it . be happy more than you be sad and being overjoyed .

you come to the way you where you desire for something new and more even than it is . you need to choose the way you wanted to may it be a tunnel or the way for your dreams but many ways and roads open for you when you will be confused in certain situations you need to cope up with those and you need to select the right one and which will give you right direction ayou come to the way you where you desire for something new and more even than it is . you need to choose the way you wanted to may it be a tunnel or the way for your dreams but many ways and roads open for you when you will be confused in certain situations you need to cope up with those and you need to select the right one and which will give you right direction ayou come to the way you where you desire for something new and more even than it is .

But from the birth only each must saying that I am different and unique from allEveryone has a spark This is thing is unit to show that to all that you are a star and you can also Shine whole world sees u have that right to Shine that right to show to That you are Better even can be best.But from the birth only each must saying that I am different and unique from allEveryone has a spark This is thing is unit to show that to all that you are a star and you can also Shine whole world sees u have that right to Shine that right to show to That you are Better even can be best.But from the birth only each must saying that I am different and unique from allEveryone has a spark This is thing is unit to show that to all that you are a star and you can also Shine whole world sees u have that right to Shine that right to show to That you are Better even can be best.But from the birth only each must saying that I am different and unique from all.

You are the Ones will Shine most pregnant one from the all and you can show to all that you are the best one. Each one thing that certain things must happen in his life but will not happen ultimately. You are the Ones will Shine most pregnant one from the all and you can show to all that you are the best one. Each one thing that certain things must happen in his life but will not happen ultimately. You are the Ones will Shine most pregnant one from the all and you can show to all that you are the best one. Each one thing that certain things must happen in his life but will not happen ultimately.

VIII

What is failure?

We all have have some good people in our lives while some as per a person we dont think that the person is good , it is a part of our thinking what I want to share actually is thatsome people take us to bright path while some address us to dark path even though they are aware with it thatthe path that person is on is not good for him/her but still if one guides that is not a good habit that actually one should have each one must be with different habits , different talents , different creativities but that should not harm anybody not that person too nor others even if we look forward for it the most important thing that each one knows even each one has experienced it . that s our perspective , our vision towards anything that we are looking for whatever thing we want to achieve in our lives we need to work for that . so as our life is with many unexpected problems and people some will take to bright path while some will go with dark one and suggest others the dark because some people rather I would say many people think that why he is happy not why I am sad but why he is happy so certain situations take place in our lives that even we dont want that to happen but excpectedly that happens so we ned to overcome with it . so in our goal dream to success many obstacles are going to come with that many failures will bring up there but these failures are only the steping stones to success.

Here I want to share my incident with you all I am talking about my present incident that just happened with me before few weeks my half yearly exam were going on and it was navratri festival going on I think it was 7th or 8th day of navratri and it was all rush at my home and after that night my english exam was there from morning it seemed to me as I was on fast I havent ate anything and then as I came home I got ready for coaching classes and I departed from my home at 4:30 without having food as I reached classes I started to feel hungry and weak then after two period I was feeling very weak then my teacher called my father and then I went to hospital then the doctor said that I was having fever then I was hospitilized for that night at next day morning but that days my english exam was there which I was unable to give then thats what I got passing marks in that subject and I was not able to score good in exam so some times such situations evn come to you where you are willing to do that but some conditions are there which wont help you .

As result day came even I was not the topper and in top three my name was not there still all my teachers and most important my parents they supported me and they didnt let me down in that situations . My class teacher rather my philosopher respected surj sir he is the one due to whom I was able to come out from that phase of failure and his words always inspired me to do not only good but best .It is not only related to study but overall development . when my result was there I didnt attended it my parents attended it but when they came from my school they were happy I was even surpised that time as I knew that my result was not so good . that day they told me that your other subjects results were excellent so you must be seeing that what is good in that not what is lacking behind . even I got a true inspiration in surj sir for many things the best I got is to not limit ourselves and to be unlimited it means that we must not limit ourselves that I can only do that but our mind aim must be that we can do many more things and again that is very importnat in each ones life is to accept the truth really words are not there for such great personality hats off to you sir...

Failure is the state or condition of not meeting a desirable or intended objective, and may be viewed as the opposite of success.The criteria for failure depends on context, and may be relative to a particular observer or belief system. One person might consider a failure what another person considers a success, particularly in cases of direct competition or a zero-sum game. Similarly, the degree of success or failure in a situation may be differently viewed by distinct observers or participants, such that a situation that one considers to be a failure, another might consider to be a success, a qualified success or a neutral situation.

It may also be difficult or impossible to ascertain whether a situation meets criteria for failure or success due to ambiguous or ill-defined definition of those criteria. Finding useful and effective criteria, or heuristics, to judge the success or failure of a situation may itself be a significant task.Cultural historian Scott Sandage argues that the concept of failure underwent a metamorphosis in the United States over the course of the 19th century. Initially, Sandage notes, financial failure, or bankruptcy, was understood as an event in a person's life: an occurrence, not a character trait. The notion of a person being a failure, Sandage argues, is a relative historical novelty: "[n]ot until the eve of the Civil War did Americans commonly label an insolvent man 'a failure'"

A failing grade is a mark or grade given to a student to indicate that they did not pass an assignment or a class. Grades may be given as numbers, letters or other symbols. By the year 1884, Mount Holyoke College was evaluating students' performance on a 100-point or percentage scale and then summarizing those numerical grades by assigning letter grades to numerical ranges. Mount Holyoke assigned letter grades A through E, with E indicating lower than 75% performance and designating failure. The A–E system spread to Harvard University by 1890. In 1898, Mount Holyoke adjusted the grading system, adding an F grade for failing (and adjusting the ranges corresponding to the other letters). The practice of letter grades spread more broadly in the first decades of the 20th century. By the 1930s, the letter E was dropped from the system, for unclear reasons.

Marketing researchers have distinguished between outcome and process failures. An outcome failure is a failure to obtain a good or service at all; a process failure is a failure to receive the good or service in an appropriate or preferable way. Thus, a person who is only interested in the final outcome of an activity would consider it to be an outcome failure if the core issue has not been resolved or a core need is not met. A process failure occurs, by contrast, when, although the activity is completed successfully, the customer still perceives the way in which the activity is conducted to be below an expected standard or benchmark.

Philosophers in the analytic tradition have suggested that failure is connected to the notion of an omission. Both actions and omissions may be morally significant. The classic example of a morally significant omission is one's failure to rescue someone in dire need of assistance. It may seem that one is morally blameworthy for failing to rescue in such a case.

Scientific hypotheses can be said to fail when they lead to predictions that do not match the results found in experiments. Alternatively, experiments can be regarded as failures when they do not provide helpful information about nature. However, the standards of what constitutes failure are not clear-cut. For example, the Michelson–Morley experiment became the "most famous failed experiment in history" because it did not detect the motion of the Earth through the luminiferous aether as had been expected. This failure to confirm the presence of the aether would later provide support for Albert Einstein's special theory of relativity. The wisdom of learning from failure is incontrovertible. Yet organizations that do it well are extraordinarily rare. This gap is not due to a lack of commitment to learning. Managers in the vast majority of enterprises that I have studied over the past 20 years—pharmaceutical, financial services, product design, telecommunications, and construction companies; hospitals; and NASA's space shuttle program, among others—genuinely wanted to help their organizations learn from failures to improve future performance. In some cases they and their teams had devoted many hours to after-action reviews, postmortems, and the like. But time after time I saw that these painstaking efforts led to no real change. The reason: Those managers were thinking about failure the wrong way.

Most executives I've talked to believe that failure is bad (of course!). They also believe that learning from it is pretty straightforward: Ask people to reflect on what they did wrong and exhort them to avoid similar mistakes in the future—or, better yet, assign a team to review and write a report on what happened and then distribute it throughout the organization.

These widely held beliefs are misguided. First, failure is not always bad. In organizational life it is sometimes bad, sometimes inevitable, and sometimes even good. Second, learning from organizational failures is anything but straightforward. The attitudes and activities required to effectively detect and analyze failures are in short supply in most companies, and the need for context-specific learning strategies is underappreciated. Organizations need new and better ways to go beyond lessons that are superficial ("Procedures weren't followed") or self-serving ("The market just wasn't ready for our great new product"). That means jettisoning old cultural beliefs and stereotypical notions of success and embracing failure's lessons.

Failure and fault are virtually inseparable in most households, organizations, and cultures. Every child learns at some point that admitting failure means taking the blame. That is why so few organizations have shifted to a culture of psychological safety in which the rewards of learning from failure can be fully realized.

Executives I've interviewed in organizations as different as hospitals and investment banks admit to being torn: How can they respond constructively to failures without giving rise to an anything-goes attitude? If people aren't blamed for failures, what will ensure that they try as hard as possible to do their best work?

This concern is based on a false dichotomy. In actuality, a culture that makes it safe to admit and report on failure can—and in some organizational contexts must—coexist with high standards for performance. To understand why, look at the exhibit "A Spectrum of Reasons for Failure," which lists causes ranging from deliberate deviation to thoughtful experimentation.

Which of these causes involve blameworthy actions? Deliberate deviance, first on the list, obviously warrants blame. But inattention might not. If it results from a lack of effort, perhaps it's blameworthy. But if it results from fatigue near the end of an overly long shift, the manager who assigned the shift is more at fault than the employee. As we go down the list, it gets more and more difficult to find blameworthy acts. In fact, a failure resulting from thoughtful experimentation that generates valuable information may actually be praiseworthy.

When I ask executives to consider this spectrum and then to estimate how many of the failures in their organizations are truly blameworthy, their answers are usually in single digits—perhaps 2% to 5%. But when I ask how many are treated as blameworthy, they say (after a pause or a laugh)

70% to 90%. The unfortunate consequence is that many failures go unreported and their lessons are lost.

Most failures in this category can indeed be considered "bad." They usually involve deviations from spec in the closely defined processes of high-volume or routine operations in manufacturing and services. With proper training and support, employees can follow those processes consistently. When they don't, deviance, inattention, or lack of ability is usually the reason. But in such cases, the causes can be readily identified and solutions developed. Checklists (as in the Harvard surgeon Atul Gawande's recent best seller The Checklist Manifesto) are one solution. Another is the vaunted Toyota Production System, which builds continual learning from tiny failures (small process deviations) into its approach to improvement. As most students of operations know well, a team member on a Toyota assembly line who spots a problem or even a potential problem is encouraged to pull a rope called the andon cord, which immediately initiates a diagnostic and problem-solving process. Production continues unimpeded if the problem can be remedied in less than a minute. Otherwise, production is halted—despite the loss of revenue entailed—until the failure is understood and resolved.

Most failures in this category can indeed be considered "bad." They usually involve deviations from spec in the closely defined processes of high-volume or routine operations in manufacturing and services. With proper training and support, employees can follow those processes consistently. When they don't, deviance, inattention, or lack of ability is usually the reason. But in such cases, the causes can be readily identified and solutions developed. Checklists (as in the Harvard surgeon Atul Gawande's recent best seller The Checklist Manifesto) are one solution. Another is the vaunted Toyota Production System, which builds continual learning from tiny failures (small process deviations) into its approach to improvement. As most students of operations know well, a team member on a Toyota assembly line who spots a problem or even a potential problem is encouraged to pull a rope called the andon cord, which immediately initiates a diagnostic and problem-solving process. Production continues unimpeded if the problem can be remedied in less than a minute. Otherwise, production is halted—despite the loss of revenue entailed—until the failure is understood and resolved.

A large number of organizational failures are due to the inherent uncertainty of work: A particular combination of needs, people, and problems may have never occurred before. Triaging patients in a hospital emergency room, responding to enemy actions on the battlefield, and running a fast-growing start-up all occur in unpredictable situations. And in complex organizations like aircraft carriers and nuclear power plants, system failure is a perpetual risk.

Although serious failures can be averted by following best practices for safety and risk management, including a thorough analysis of any such events that do occur, small process failures are inevitable. To consider them bad is not just a misunderstanding of how complex systems work; it is counterproductive. Avoiding consequential failures means rapidly identifying and correcting small failures. Most accidents in hospitals result from a series of small failures that went unnoticed and unfortunately lined up in just the wrong way.

Failures in this category can rightly be considered "good," because they provide valuable new knowledge that can help an organization leap ahead of the competition and ensure its future growth—which is why the Duke University professor of management Sim Sitkin calls them intelligent failures. They occur when experimentation is necessary: when answers are not knowable in advance because this exact situation hasn't been encountered before and perhaps never will be again. Discovering new drugs, creating a radically new business, designing an innovative product, and testing customer reactions in a brand-new market are tasks that require intelligent failures. "Trial and error" is a common term for the kind of experimentation needed in these settings, but it is a misnomer, because "error" implies that there was a "right" outcome in the first place. At the frontier, the right kind of experimentation produces good failures quickly. Managers who practice it can avoid the unintelligent failure of conducting experiments at a larger scale than necessary.

Leaders of the product design firm IDEO understood this when they launched a new innovation-strategy service. Rather than help clients design new products within their existing lines—a process IDEO had all but perfected—the service would help them create new lines that would take them in novel strategic directions. Knowing that it hadn't yet figured out how to deliver the service effectively, the company started a small project with a mattress company and didn't publicly announce the launch of a new business.

Only leaders can create and reinforce a culture that counteracts the blame game and makes people feel both comfortable with and responsible for surfacing and learning from failures. (See the sidebar "How Leaders Can Build a Psychologically Safe Environment.") They should insist that their organizations develop a clear understanding of what happened—not of "who did it"—when things go wrong. This requires consistently reporting failures, small and large; systematically analyzing them; and proactively searching for opportunities to experiment.

Often one context or one kind of work dominates the culture of an enterprise and shapes how it treats failure. For instance, automotive companies, with their predictable, high-volume operations, understandably tend to view failure as something that can and should be prevented. But most organizations engage in all three kinds of work discussed above—routine, complex, and frontier. Leaders must ensure that the right approach to learning from failure is applied in each. All organizations learn from failure through three essential activities: detection, analysis, and experimentation.

Spotting big, painful, expensive failures is easy. But in many organizations any failure that can be hidden is hidden as long as it's unlikely to cause immediate or obvious harm. The goal should be to surface it early, before it has mushroomed into disaster.

Shortly after arriving from Boeing to take the reins at Ford, in September 2006, Alan Mulally instituted a new system for detecting failures. He asked managers to color code their reports green for good, yellow for caution, or red for problems—a common management technique. According to a 2009 story in Fortune, at his first few meetings all the managers coded their operations green, to Mulally's frustration. Reminding them that the company had lost several billion dollars the previous year, he asked straight out, "Isn't anything not going well?" After one tentative yellow report was made about a serious product defect that would probably delay a launch, Mulally responded to the deathly silence that ensued with applause. After that, the weekly staff meetings were full of color.

That story illustrates a pervasive and fundamental problem: Although many methods of surfacing current and pending failures exist, they are grossly underutilized. Total Quality

Management and soliciting feedback from customers are well-known techniques for bringing to light failures in routine operations. High-reliability-organization (HRO) practices help prevent catastrophic failures in complex systems like nuclear power plants through early detection. Electricité de France, which operates 58 nuclear power plants, has been an exemplar in this area: It goes beyond regulatory requirements and religiously tracks each plant for anything even slightly out of the ordinary, immediately investigates whatever turns up, and informs all its other plants of any anomalies.

Such methods are not more widely employed because all too many messengers—even the most senior executives—remain reluctant to convey bad news to bosses and colleagues. One senior executive I know in a large consumer products company had grave reservations about a takeover that was already in the works when he joined the management team. But, overly conscious of his newcomer status, he was silent during discussions in which all the other executives seemed enthusiastic about the plan. Many months later, when the takeover had clearly failed, the team gathered to review what had happened. Aided by a consultant, each executive considered what he or she might have done to contribute to the failure. The newcomer, openly apologetic about his past silence, explained that others' enthusiasm had made him unwilling to be "the skunk at the picnic."

In researching errors and other failures in hospitals, I discovered substantial differences across patient-care units in nurses' willingness to speak up about them. It turned out that the behavior of midlevel managers—how they responded to failures and whether they encouraged open discussion of them, welcomed questions, and displayed humility and curiosity—was the cause. I have seen the same pattern in a wide range of organizations.

A horrific case in point, which I studied for more than two years, is the 2003 explosion of the Columbia space shuttle, which killed seven astronauts (see "Facing Ambiguous Threats," by Michael A. Roberto, Richard M.J. Bohmer, and Amy C. Edmondson, HBR November 2006). NASA managers spent some two weeks downplaying the seriousness of a piece of foam's having broken off the left side of the shuttle at launch. They rejected engineers' requests to resolve the ambiguity (which could have been done by having a satellite photograph the shuttle or asking the astronauts to conduct a space walk to inspect the area in question), and the major failure went largely undetected until its fatal consequences 16 days later. Ironically, a shared but unsubstantiated belief among program managers that there was little they could do contributed to their inability to detect the failure. Postevent analyses suggested that they might indeed have taken fruitful action. But clearly leaders hadn't established the necessary culture, systems, and procedures.

One challenge is teaching people in an organization when to declare defeat in an experimental course of action. The human tendency to hope for the best and try to avoid failure at all costs gets in the way, and organizational hierarchies exacerbate it. As a result, failing R&D projects are often kept going much longer than is scientifically rational or economically prudent. We throw good money after bad, praying that we'll pull a rabbit out of a hat. Intuition may tell engineers or scientists that a project has fatal flaws, but the formal decision to call it a failure may be delayed for months.

Once a failure has been detected, it's essential to go beyond the obvious and superficial reasons for it to understand the root causes. This requires the discipline—better yet, the enthusiasm—to use sophisticated analysis to ensure that the right lessons are learned and the right remedies are employed. The job of leaders is to see that their organizations don't just move on after a failure but stop to dig in and discover the wisdom contained in it.

Why is failure analysis often shortchanged? Because examining our failures in depth is emotionally unpleasant and can chip away at our self-esteem. Left to our own devices, most of us will speed through or avoid failure analysis altogether. Another reason is that analyzing organizational failures requires inquiry and openness, patience, and a tolerance for causal ambiguity. Yet managers typically admire and are rewarded for decisiveness, efficiency, and action—not thoughtful reflection. That is why the right culture is so important.

The challenge is more than emotional; it's cognitive, too. Even without meaning to, we all favor evidence that supports our existing beliefs rather than alternative explanations. We also tend to downplay our responsibility and place undue blame on external or situational factors when we fail, only to do the reverse when assessing the failures of others—a psychological trap known as fundamental attribution error.

My research has shown that failure analysis is often limited and ineffective—even in complex organizations like hospitals, where human lives are at stake. Few hospitals systematically analyze medical errors or process flaws in order to capture failure's lessons. Recent research in North Carolina hospitals, published in November 2010 in the New England Journal of Medicine, found that despite a dozen years of heightened awareness that medical errors result in thousands of deaths each year, hospitals have not become safer.

Fortunately, there are shining exceptions to this pattern, which continue to provide hope that organizational learning is possible. At Intermountain Healthcare, a system of 23 hospitals that serves Utah and southeastern Idaho, physicians' deviations from medical protocols are routinely analyzed for opportunities to improve the protocols. Allowing deviations and sharing the data on whether they actually produce a better outcome encourages physicians to buy into this program. (See "Fixing Health Care on the Front Lines," by Richard M.J. Bohmer, HBR April 2010.)

Motivating people to go beyond first-order reasons (procedures weren't followed) to understanding the second- and third-order reasons can be a major challenge. One way to do this is to use interdisciplinary teams with diverse skills and perspectives. Complex failures in particular are the result of multiple events that occurred in different departments or disciplines or at different levels of the organization. Understanding what happened and how to prevent it from happening again requires detailed, team-based discussion and analysis.

A team of leading physicists, engineers, aviation experts, naval leaders, and even astronauts devoted months to an analysis of the Columbia disaster. They conclusively established not only the first-order cause—a piece of foam had hit the shuttle's leading edge during launch—but also second-order causes: A rigid hierarchy and schedule-obsessed culture at NASA made it especially difficult for engineers to speak up about anything but the most rock-solid concerns.

Once a failure has been detected, it's essential to go beyond the obvious and superficial reasons for it to understand the root causes. This requires the discipline—better yet, the enthusiasm—to use sophisticated analysis to ensure that the right lessons are learned and the right remedies are employed. The job of leaders is to see that their organizations don't just move on after a failure but stop to dig in and discover the wisdom contained in it.

Why is failure analysis often shortchanged? Because examining our failures in depth is emotionally unpleasant and can chip away at our self-esteem. Left to our own devices, most of us will speed through or avoid failure analysis altogether. Another reason is that analyzing organizational failures requires inquiry and openness, patience, and a tolerance for causal ambiguity. Yet managers typically admire and are rewarded for decisiveness, efficiency, and action—not thoughtful reflection. That is why the right culture is so important.

The challenge is more than emotional; it's cognitive, too. Even without meaning to, we all favor evidence that supports our existing beliefs rather than alternative explanations. We also tend to downplay our responsibility and place undue blame on external or situational factors when we fail, only to do the reverse when assessing the failures of others—a psychological trap known as fundamental attribution error.

My research has shown that failure analysis is often limited and ineffective—even in complex organizations like hospitals, where human lives are at stake. Few hospitals systematically analyze medical errors or process flaws in order to capture failure's lessons. Recent research in North Carolina hospitals, published in November 2010 in the New England Journal of Medicine, found that despite a dozen years of heightened awareness that medical errors result in thousands of deaths each year, hospitals have not become safer.

Fortunately, there are shining exceptions to this pattern, which continue to provide hope that organizational learning is possible. At Intermountain Healthcare, a system of 23 hospitals that serves Utah and southeastern Idaho, physicians' deviations from medical protocols are routinely analyzed for opportunities to improve the protocols. Allowing deviations and sharing the data on whether they actually produce a better outcome encourages physicians to buy into this program. (See "Fixing Health Care on the Front Lines," by Richard M.J. Bohmer, HBR April 2010.)

Motivating people to go beyond first-order reasons (procedures weren't followed) to understanding the second- and third-order reasons can be a major challenge. One way to do this is to use interdisciplinary teams with diverse skills and perspectives. Complex failures in particular are the result of multiple events that occurred in different departments or disciplines or at different levels of the organization. Understanding what happened and how to prevent it from happening again requires detailed, team-based discussion and analysis.

A team of leading physicists, engineers, aviation experts, naval leaders, and even astronauts devoted months to an analysis of the Columbia disaster. They conclusively established not only the first-order cause—a piece of foam had hit the shuttle's leading edge during launch—but also second-order causes: A rigid hierarchy and schedule-obsessed culture at NASA made it especially difficult for engineers to speak up about anything but the most rock-solid concerns.

The third critical activity for effective learning is strategically producing failures—in the right places, at the right times—through systematic experimentation. Researchers in basic science know that although the experiments they conduct will occasionally result in a spectacular success, a large percentage of them (70% or higher in some fields) will fail. How do these people get out of bed in the morning? First, they know that failure is not optional in their work; it's part of being at the leading edge of scientific discovery. Second, far more than most of us, they understand that every failure conveys valuable information, and they're eager to get it before the competition does.

In contrast, managers in charge of piloting a new product or service—a classic example of experimentation in business—typically do whatever they can to make sure that the pilot is perfect right out of the starting gate. Ironically, this hunger to succeed can later inhibit the success of the official launch. Too often, managers in charge of pilots design optimal conditions rather than representative ones. Thus the pilot doesn't produce knowledge about what won't work.

The third critical activity for effective learning is strategically producing failures—in the right places, at the right times—through systematic experimentation. Researchers in basic science know that although the experiments they conduct will occasionally result in a spectacular success, a large percentage of them (70% or higher in some fields) will fail. How do these people get out of bed in the morning? First, they know that failure is not optional in their work; it's part of being at the leading edge of scientific discovery. Second, far more than most of us, they understand that every failure conveys valuable information, and they're eager to get it before the competition does.

In contrast, managers in charge of piloting a new product or service—a classic example of experimentation in business—typically do whatever they can to make sure that the pilot is perfect right out of the starting gate. Ironically, this hunger to succeed can later inhibit the success of the official launch. Too often, managers in charge of pilots design optimal conditions rather than representative ones. Thus the pilot doesn't produce knowledge about what won't work.

n the very early days of DSL, a major telecommunications company I'll call Telco did a full-scale launch of that high-speed technology to consumer households in a major urban market. It was an unmitigated customer-service disaster. The company missed 75% of its commitments and found itself confronted with a staggering 12,000 late orders. Customers were frustrated and upset, and service reps couldn't even begin to answer all their calls. Employee morale suffered. How could this happen to a leading company with high satisfaction ratings and a brand that had long stood for excellence?

A small and extremely successful suburban pilot had lulled Telco executives into a misguided confidence. The problem was that the pilot did not resemble real service conditions: It was staffed with unusually personable, expert service reps and took place in a community of educated, tech-savvy customers. But DSL was a brand-new technology and, unlike traditional telephony, had to interface with customers' highly variable home computers and technical skills. This added complexity and unpredictability to the service-delivery challenge in ways that Telco had not fully appreciated before the launch.

A more useful pilot at Telco would have tested the technology with limited support, unsophisticated customers, and old computers. It would have been designed to discover everything that could go wrong—instead of proving that under the best of conditions everything would go right. (See the sidebar "Designing Successful Failures.") Of course, the managers in charge would have to have understood that they were going to be rewarded not for success but, rather, for producing intelligent failures as quickly as possible.

n the very early days of DSL, a major telecommunications company I'll call Telco did a full-scale launch of that high-speed technology to consumer households in a major urban market. It was an unmitigated customer-service disaster. The company missed 75% of its commitments and found itself confronted with a staggering 12,000 late orders. Customers were frustrated and upset, and service reps couldn't even begin to answer all their calls. Employee morale suffered. How could this happen to a leading company with high satisfaction ratings and a brand that had long stood for excellence?

A small and extremely successful suburban pilot had lulled Telco executives into a misguided confidence. The problem was that the pilot did not resemble real service conditions: It was staffed with unusually personable, expert service reps and took place in a community of educated, tech-savvy customers. But DSL was a brand-new technology and, unlike traditional telephony, had to interface with customers' highly variable home computers and technical skills. This added complexity and unpredictability to the service-delivery challenge in ways that Telco had not fully appreciated before the launch.

A more useful pilot at Telco would have tested the technology with limited support, unsophisticated customers, and old computers. It would have been designed to discover everything that could go wrong—instead of proving that under the best of conditions everything would go right. (See the sidebar "Designing Successful Failures.") Of course, the managers in charge would have to have understood that they were going to be rewarded not for success but, rather, for producing intelligent failures as quickly as possible.

In short, exceptional organizations are those that go beyond detecting and analyzing failures and try to generate intelligent ones for the express purpose of learning and innovating. It's not that managers in these organizations enjoy failure. But they recognize it as a necessary by-product of experimentation. They also realize that they don't have to do dramatic experiments with large budgets. Often a small pilot, a dry run of a new technique, or a simulation will suffice.

The courage to confront our own and others' imperfections is crucial to solving the apparent contradiction of wanting neither to discourage the reporting of problems nor to create an environment in which anything goes. This means that managers must ask employees to be brave and speak up—and must not respond by expressing anger or strong disapproval of what may at first appear to be incompetence. More often than we realize, complex systems are at work behind organizational failures, and their lessons and improvement opportunities are lost when conversation is stifled.

In short, exceptional organizations are those that go beyond detecting and analyzing failures and try to generate intelligent ones for the express purpose of learning and innovating. It's not that managers in these organizations enjoy failure. But they recognize it as a necessary by-product of experimentation. They also realize that they don't have to do dramatic experiments with large budgets. Often a small pilot, a dry run of a new technique, or a simulation will suffice.

The courage to confront our own and others' imperfections is crucial to solving the apparent contradiction of wanting neither to discourage the reporting of problems nor to create an environment in which anything goes. This means that managers must ask employees to be brave and speak up—and must not respond by expressing anger or strong disapproval of what may at first appear to be incompetence. More often than we realize, complex systems are at work behind organizational failures, and their lessons and improvement opportunities are lost when conversation is stifled.

IX

Failure is first step to success

Whenever I FAIL to do something it may be not with studies still one person who always guided to do good my parents are always the first one but beside them if I talk about then it is Abhijeet sir.he is the one who always helped in my creative works and appreciated it his words always gave impact on students . I t was really very sad day for me when the last time abhijeet sir talked with me in school that he is going to leave the school for somewhere I felt that now what will happen to the students of abhijeet sir but really the each thing he did for each one is memorable and remarkable .

here I want to add his words on our topic Failure is first step to success. So it is said by Abhijeet Sir" We all have observed that since childhood failure starts as child tries to walk. But journey from crawl to walk and walk to run itself is a success. Life proceeds in a same way. It is saying that, "Everything feels impossible in the beginning." But if a person doesn't give up and learn from the failure so definitely one can achieve desired results.

Remember we fail, we learn and we grow up. It is continuous

process.

As I red somewhere that FEAR has two meanings. Fear Everything And Run and Face Everything And Rise. So it is very important to rise again after falling down because when you are lifting yourself up again that time you have experience of failure and that experience of failure will guide you that which mistake should not be repeated. The former president of America Mr. Abraham Lincoln is the best example to take motivation. After failing several times he didn't give up. He made all his failures a staircase towards success and conquered the place of president of USA at the age of 54. The one who invented bulb, Mr. Thomas Edison has failed more than 1000 times but at the end finished with the greatest ever invention."his words are always relastic, amazing and astonishing . I salute to his writting skill andworld of imagination.

Do you know that failure is the first step to success? Though we've been conditioned to avoid failure at all costs, it's actually the one thing that will lead to success. As counterintuitive as this concept may seem, it's proven itself to be true countless times.

1. Failure teaches lessons that you wouldn't learn otherwise

In general, some of life's greatest lessons are best learned through experience rather than theory. For example, you may tell a child not to touch a hot stove and they may listen.

But, if they touch a hot stove, they'll immediately experience the unpleasant feeling of burning themselves and its consequences. These are both lessons from life experiments they would not have learned otherwise.

This is exactly how failure works. Although it may seem unpleasant and uncomfortable, it gives your an experience that theory can't do. With that in mind, some lessons only come from failure—making failure one of the greatest teachers.

2. You learn what not to do the next time

What is another reason failure is the first step to success? Failure gives you experiences that you can apply the next time you try. This means that you can avoid the same pitfalls that hindered you from initially reaching your goal. A simple example of this is getting lost while driving. One wrong turn can take you far away from your intended destination—causing you time and frustration. However, the next time you venture to that destination, you'll know what paths to avoid.

3. You can use failure for motivation

For many people, failure can be a form of motivation. It sparks a desire to get back up and try again. Perhaps it may be to prove to yourself (or others) that you can do it. We see this often with sports teams who fall short of the ultimate championship victory. Postgame interviews reveal that players are motivated to come back the next year to try again. As a result, they practice more, they learn new techniques, and they prepare themselves to try again.

Likewise, you can use any failure that you experience in life to motivate yourself to become better. Ultimately, failure can reveal where you may need some improvement.Use it as motivation for the self-improvement necessary to accomplish your goals. So you see failure is the first step to success if you use it as motivation!

4.You can use your failure to can teach others

The great thing about life's lessons is that they aren't simply for you. Collectively, as the human race, we learn from the successes and failures of those around us. This allows us to grow as a society and, in some ways, shortcuts the learning process.Science is a great example of everyone benefiting from the failures of others. Every day, researchers conduct experiments that provide more information that can advance science and technology.Much of this includes failed experiments that teach us new things that we wouldn't learn otherwise. This becomes shared knowledge that we can use to advance society.

Sharing our failures with others can allow them to avoid mistakes we've made so that they can reach their goals much sooner. So don't be ashamed of not reaching your goals if it can help someone reach theirs. Your failure is the first step to success for others as well.

Don't give up because failure is the first step to success! The average person experiences failure time and time again. But as you can see, failure really isn't the end. Instead, failure is the first step to success — whatever that looks like for you. It's an opportunity to grow, improve, and help others along the way. But in order for it to be a path to success, you must reshape your view of failure and its role in your life.

Even people come across different circumstances that they are actually very near to success and they are about to achieve the victory but because of obsatcles they are unable to success in thier lives , life gives you opportunity

X

From the known movie

Chhichore short story of movie

Anirudh "Anni" Pathak is a divorced middle-aged man living with his teenage son Raghav Pathak, an aspiring engineer, who is awaiting the results of his entrance examination in the hope of enrolling in the Indian Institute of Technology. On the eve of the results, Anni gifts Raghav a bottle of champagne, promising him that they will celebrate his success together, unaware that Raghav is under intense pressure. The bottle of champagne only fuels Raghav's worries as to what will happen if he does not make it. The next day, while checking the results at his friend's apartment, Raghav finds out that he has not qualified for IIT-JEE exam results and, afraid of being called a "loser", he deliberately slips off the balcony to commit suicide, but survives, although in a fatal state. Anni rushes to the hospital where he tries to comfort his ex-wife Maya Pathak. She blames Anni for not noticing how much pressure Raghav was in. Dr. Sunit Dev "S. D." Kasbekar informs Maya and Anni that Raghav's condition is deteriorating as Raghav does not have the will to live. Realizing that his son is afraid of being called a "loser", Anni, who stumbles upon pictures of his college days, begins to recount the tales of his time in college in an attempt to rekindle hope in Raghav, who he wants to believe that his father, too, was once a "loser".

During the recount, the story flashes back to 1992 when it was his first day of college at the National College of Technology campus. Anni is allotted a room in Hostel 4 a.k.a. "H4", which is famous for housing "losers". The occupants of H4 have earned this tag for numerous unknown reasons, one of them being the poorest quality of mess food on the entire campus. Dissatisfied, he applies to change his hostel block although a clerk informs him that his application might take time. Meanwhile, a senior H4 student Gurmeet "Sexa" Singh Dhillon pokes Anni in the butt the first time they meet, but they soon become friends, with Anni describing Sexa as a hyper-sexual senior who was obsessed with pornography all the time.

At this point, Raghav has a convulsion, causing Anni and Maya to panic, but Dr. Kasbekar reveals that he is now conscious, though his condition is still the same. When he asks about "Sexa", though, Anni, convinced that Raghav was listening, goes in with Maya to meet Raghav, who doubts if it is indeed a true story. Anni, convinced that he just needs proof to make his plan work, eventually traces Sexa, who is currently working as a consultant in London, through a call, and informs him about the tragedy. Sexa postpones his work commitments and flies down to Mumbai to reunite with Anni and Maya, and seeing Sexa, an initially dismayed Raghav recognizes him and puts all his doubts to rest, as Sexa continues with the story.

Sexa narrates Anni's desperation to change his hostel, and in 1992, during their initial conversation at a canteen, they notice Maya for the first time.

As the story returns to the present, Sexa narrates to Anni and Maya during a lunch break how he and a friend named Himanshu "Acid" Deshmukh once received a funny pro-ragging request in 1992 from the father of a fresher named Sundar "Mummy" Shrivastava, a young introvert who is tied to his mother's apron strings and is very dependent on her. At this stage, Mummy joins Sexa in the present-day, working as an executive in the United States, which has thickened his accent. When both Anni and Sexa spill news of Acid's arrival, Mummy exclaims to Raghav that Acid is "bad news". Anni then describes Acid as a school topper who began flunking his college tests and developed a bitter, swearing tongue. A brief introduction for Acid soon pans back to Sexa's classmate joining them in the hospital. All of them briefly reminisce the fun they had in their college days, showing their photo album to Raghav and telling him about Anni's newfound relationship with Maya back then, even as Dr. Kasbekar, time and again, informs them that Raghav's brain is swelling, and his condition doesn't show signs of improvement.

Meanwhile, back in 1992, a super-senior student named Raghuvir "Raggie" Chalkar, a reputed hostelite of Hostel 3 a.k.a. "H3", which is known to be a world-class hostel and the absolute antithesis of H4, fast-tracks Anni's application and offers him to come to H3, but Anni has a sudden change of heart while discussing this with Maya, later rejecting the offer, much to the chagrin of Raggie, who reveals that H4 super-senior Derek D'Souza, a well-known athlete, has been "rotting" for the past three years after having similarly rejected a previous offer.

Derek is revealed to be a chain smoker, and as he reunites with Anni, a scene of their first meeting back in 1992 plays out, wherein Derek reveals that Raggie is a full-blown college bully who inducts talented students from other hostels into

H3 and claims total credit for winning "GC". An initially surprised Anni soon learns that H4's "loser" status comes from its consistently worst performances over the years in the "GC", which stands for General Championship, an annual sports competition whence students of all 10 hostels of the entire institute compete in 30 sports over a span of 2 months. Anni then convinces an initially sceptical Derek to try for one last time, and they begin a series of trials, hilariously failing in the bargain. After multiple attempts to find the right players fail, Derek gives the same reply to Anni as one that Dr. Kasbekar gives to him and Maya - that it has to be all about trying, for there's no other way.

Back at Anni's house, everyone is having a discussion, where Derek, Acid, Sexa, and Mummy tell Anni and Maya that they'll be sticking around to support them after Anni requests them to leave due to the negative reports of Raghav's health, when just before everyone can assemble for dinner on the dining table, Anni and the "losers" find their long-missing member, Sahil "Bevda" Awasthi, at Anni's doorstep. Bevda joins the group at the hospital the next day, and as is implied, he is shown to be the "Devdas-inspired drunkard" of the group, also a known chess champion.

They then recount that while preparing for the GC back in 1992, as they lose an initial string of matches in different sports, except carrom tournaments where Mummy leads them to the quarter-finals, all six boys decide to sacrifice things closest to them until they win the GC. Anni, in his bid, decides to temporarily boycott Maya, avoiding her constantly. However, this tactic hits back severely on their faces when Bevda has a relapse and is taken to hospital, causing the H4 team to lose hope. However, after a moment of introspection, Anni soon comes up with a trifecta of plans to defeat other hostels. His methods work, resulting in several massive victories for H4. During a celebration hangout at a bar, however, a violent clash between Raggie's gang and the leading losers culminates in Mummy injuring his finger, causing Mummy to lose the carrom semi-finals. Even as Acid consoles a crying Mummy, lack of representation in a weightlifting tournament instantly strikes an idea in Anni's head and he chooses Abhimanyu "Danda" Rathore, an H4 hostelite, to lose 2 kgs through training under Anni and Derek's supervision and compete in the 42 kg category. His hilarious victory is soon accompanied by Bewda's return from rehab, which the hostel celebrates. Bevda continues to reign in points for H4 in chess after his return, Derek's athletic skills prove a great asset for H4, and eventually, H4 makes it to the finals, pitted against H3, for the first time in college history.

Back in the present, Dr. Kasbekar asks Anni, Maya, and their friends to leave Raghav at this point, so that he can have his surgical operation done the next morning, and they all promise Raghav to wait patiently for the "climax". After the friends return to Anni's home, the friends have a discussion where Anni reveals that he probably failed in teaching Raghav how to deal with failures, pointing to the bottle of champagne he had bought for him. Seeing Mummy call up his son Vedant and tell him that he will gift him a bike irrespective of what his exam results would be, Maya surmises that Anni is an exceptional father and reconciles with him after an emotional breakdown. Right in the middle of the night, Anni's phone suddenly rings, wherein Dr. Kasbekar informs him that Raghav has had severe convulsions, and an immediate operation would have to be carried out. Anni requests 10 minutes for finishing the story, and Dr. Kasbekar, initially reluctant, gives in after Maya supports him.

They resume the story, where back in 1992, a vexed Raggie, upon learning of H4's methods, decides to sabotage Bevda by offering him a bottle of alcohol, and deliberately has his teammate injure Derek's foot. Bevda initially appears to be drunk when Anni and Sexa are to receive him, and after Anni departs for the basketball final, tends to move towards a loss in the game, when he suddenly reveals that he isn't drunk and that he had let his opponent make a huge mistake sacrificing his knight. Eventually, with both Acid and Derek winning the relay final, Bevda also wins the chess tournament. They reunite with Anni at the basketball court, and while Anni gets a penalty shot and aims for a 3-pointer, his shot misses by almost an inch, causing H4 to lose the GC by a close margin.

Back in the present, Raghav is shocked at this moment of loss and asks Anni if he felt like committing suicide at that moment, having lost a battle this close. Anni, Derek, Mummy, Acid, Sexa, Bevda, and Maya take turns in replying with a "NO", as Anni then explains in a flashback to 1992 that Raggie publicly called them "champs" instead of "losers" for the first time, creating a loud wave of cheer for H4 and congratulating the team for putting up a good fight. Anni then explains to Raghav that the H4 hostelites were never called "losers" again and that it is not one's results that decide whether he or she is a "loser", but rather one's efforts. Convincing him that he tried very hard, Anni asks Raghav to put up a strong face and fight all his challenges in life, including the operation, and as he is being taken to the operation theatre, Raghav visualizes Anni, Derek, Mummy, Acid, Sexa, Bevda and Maya in their younger selves cheering him to fight on.

A year later, a fully recovered Raghav attends his first day of college, requesting the viewers to never ask what the name of his college is or what his rank was since he is content that he is getting to live life and enjoy it to the maximum. As he reaches the new campus, he laughs at his senior's question as grown-up apparitions of his parents and the rest of the 'losers' look at him.

basically this movie is all about the failure story that how it was a big failure for young boy raghav one this he took or he shown sudden reaction on it as we say that every action has equal and opposite reaction and raghav reacted on it and he decided to end his life with surrender and thats what he did and he suided that day but after that he came to know the story of his father that he was a big failure and he got that he was failure in his life and thats what each one has to face in his life and that is what we get from the movie even though movie is very interesting and overwhelming

XI

we come up with failure

Failure - we all come in contact with it. And more often than not, we dread even entertaining the idea of failing. As a society, we see failure to be detrimental to our success. Ever since we are young, we are taught to avoid failure. In school, we aim to get As, so that we can get into a good university or get a good job offer after college. We avoid getting an 'F' like the plague because that would mean we failed at something. As a matter of fact, in the letter grading system, F is the only letter grade which corresponds to the first letter of what it stands for: failure. In this subtle way, the idea that failure is not good for us becomes embedded in our mind and we try to avoid it. Instead of seeing failure as a natural part of life, we see it as very negative.

Two world-renowned psychologists, Daniel Kahneman and Amos Tversky, who won the Nobel Prize for their work, which explains why we are so averse to failure. What they found is that effect of loss is twice as great as the gain from a win. This is an astounding conclusion indicates the great negative impact a loss has on us as individuals, which is much greater than the impact of a win. Thus, it explains why we as humans would go at lengths to avoid a loss or a failure.

Be committed

Through commitment, you can gain motivation to pursue success. You should make a list that includes your goal, your level of commitment to the goal and what you're willing to do to achieve that goal.Staying focused on your plan is crucial. It helps to put aside at least 15 minutes per day to think about your plan and work toward it. This will keep your goal fresh in your mind and allow you to continue focusing on it.In determining your commitment to your goal, however, it's important to ensure you have realistic expectations of yourself and the outcome. If your commitment is not paying off after a certain time, you should adjust your goal accordingly and revise any necessary steps.At times it may be helpful to ask a friend or family member for support in helping you stick to your commitments. Having someone to hold you accountable for your shortcomings and praise your success can help you stay committed to your goal.

Learn from the journey

Rather than focusing strictly on the results of your accomplishments, take notice of the small steps needed to achieve success. If you allow yourself to enjoy small victories along your journey, reaching your goal will become a new adventure each day and you will be more likely to stay on track. By doing this, you will learn new and exciting things along the way, which can help you grow as a person.

Have fun along the way

If the journey to achieve something becomes too tedious, it will be more challenging to succeed. Learning what you're capable of can be fun and exciting, so it's important to keep your goals light and fun to have an emotionally positive experience and keep moving forward without losing perspective.

Think positively

Developing a positive mindset is all about trusting yourself and your ability to succeed. It's important to replace any negative thoughts with positive ones to motivate yourself to keep trying no matter what challenges come your way.On your path to becoming successful, you're likely to learn new things and think differently than before. Your goals will not happen overnight. They will take practice and discipline to achieve, so it's vital to think about the process positively.

Change your perspective

Sometimes along the journey, you have to change your perspective to turn a challenging situation into a better one. When you're having a bad day or week, imagine instead that it's a good day or week.Give yourself the opportunity and the time to think about your situation using only positive language and see how much your day or week changes. Doing this for an extended period of time could change your entire life.

Be honest with yourself

If you find your goal is at a standstill, you might need to be honest with yourself about why that is. After you have come to an understanding, try to find a solution to push yourself toward success.Challenge yourself to step out of your comfort zone. This might mean an extra set of squats, having a conversation with a supervisor about a promotion or even signing up for a difficult college class that you hadn't considered before.

Take away distractions

Make a list of things in your life that take up your time or distract you. This could be a phone, a television show or even a person who causes you stress. Shut off your phone and put it in a different room when it's time to focus on your goal.Turn off the television and put the remote across the room. Only keep in contact with the people who make a positive impact on your life. Now is the best time to start changing habits so that you can focus on achieving success without distractions.

Count on yourself

You cannot count on others to achieve your goals for you. Your best friend cannot take a class for you. Your mother cannot get you a promotion. Your partner cannot lose extra weight for you. These are all things you must do on your own.It can be beneficial to rely on others for emotional support, but just as you have your needs, your friends and family have their own as well. It's important to hold yourself accountable to achieve your goals and make yourself happy.

Keep planning

Stick to a schedule when working on your goals. Give yourself challenges according to your personal calendar, such as "I will run a seven-minute mile by the end of the month," or "I will save $5,000 by the end of the year."Even if you do not achieve the goal, you will have your starting point in your calendar and will see progress. If you plan your goals and track them in a calendar, you will always have proof of your progress. Having something tangible is a great motivator to keep working toward success.

Avoid getting burned out

It's important to focus on your goal, but do not obsess over it. Keeping your journey productive but also fun will ensure you're motivated without overworking yourself. Sitting around and thinking about your goal all the time can cause you to burn out. Your previously fun goal becomes more like something you have to do than something you want to do. Continue to learn about how much you can grow and achieve to avoid getting burned out.

Most people obsess over how to be successful because we all want to feel like we matter.

Without achieving any success, we might look back on our life disappointed by our lack of impact on the world.

Striving to achieve a greater purpose is what keeps us fighting to survive and grow.

While you might not become an international success, your life can still have an impact on others.

The goal of achieving success will help you live a more purposeful life by pushing you to overcome obstacles, work a bit harder and pursue happiness.

Nothing will motivate you better than a fuming rage deep inside you.

So, here's your diss: You spend way too much time on unimportant tasks while pretending that you're 'researching or learning or finding motivation.' But truth is, you're slacking. And you're never going to get your act together unless you START WORKING. So, if you want to be able to pay your bills or travel the world, it's not going to happen if you never take that first step.

The silver bullet is that you need to put in the work everyday for years.It's not some Facebook ads hack. Or some magical $2000 conference.But no matter how many times people tell you that, you're still going to dig around for the secret answer.

Why?Because you don't want to put in the work.You want to be an overnight success.Not gonna happen, though.So if I were you, I'd start creating.

If you're looking for ways to be successful in life, you're not going to find it in the people around you. Unless, everyone around you is a giant success.Your mom, dad, best friend, partner, and dog don't need to approve your business ideas.Live life your way. Stop looking to others for validation that you're on the right track.Wanna know how you're on the right track?When you ask yourself, 'Am I living the life I want?'If the answer is yes, you're on the right track.If the answer is no, you've got some changes to make.Don't let outsiders cloud your thinking.People always think they know what's best for you.But only you'd know what that is.Trust yourself a bit more and you'll realize you know what you're doing.

Stop Looking for a Mentor

There's nothing wrong with mentorship. It can actually be really great for building your career.

Most people don't want mentorship though, they want someone to do all the work for them.

Entrepreneurship and being successful is all about taking ownership.

You talk a big game about wanting freedom, but when it comes to designing your first store, you ask for so much feedback.

But what you need to realize is that the best thing about entrepreneurship is that you can create your business any way you want.

And if you get a mentor to help you make decisions it's basically like having a boss oversee your work – you start to lose that freedom that you really wanted.If you constantly have people guiding you on your journey, your wins aren't really your wins and your losses aren't really your losses.If you don't take ownership of your wins and losses, you never really get that 'OMG! I DID IT!' feeling.And you also never learn from your mistakes because they weren't your mistakes in the first place.You're going to make bad decisions but you'll make some great ones too.You don't need a mentor to teach you how to be successful, especially if your goal is to live life on your own terms.

XII

Success

When I was in fifth grade, I was given an assignment in school to write a paper about success. My title was "Success is Simply Happiness." When I told that to my father at the dinner table on the night before the paper was due, he put down his fork, looked directly at me, and said, "All of my buddies in World War II did not die happy. Are you telling me they were not successful?" In my mind, I thought about changing the title to "Just Don't Die," but instead I sat in silence with the rest of my siblings, knowing this moment definitely was not happy, and thus my title, nor my paper, were a success.

I think possibly what I learned from that dinner is that success does not equal happiness, nor does happiness mean success.

Ever since then, the question about the definition of success has been in my mind. While I was a reporter for the student paper in college, I wrote an article about "What is Success?" I interviewed several students and most of them had my early childhood definition: Happiness. So I would ask them, "Are you happy when you're studying?" "Are you happy when negative circumstances happen that eventually bring happiness?" The unanimous answer was, "Hmmm."

Success blooms from failures along the journey.

"Learn to fail, or fail to learn." —Thomas Edison

There is such a huge difference between failing and being a failure. Ironically, failing makes you less of a failure. You can only grow from failing. If you're not willing to fail, you cannot innovate and make change. If you don't step through the uncertainty of making an attempt, you will never achieve success.

Failure and success are exactly the same direction.

That is why the journey is the reward, and success is taking the journey, not the end result.

Remember that each step is progress. Each step, no matter how small, gets easier than the last. Soon they will become giant strides. Each time we adapt to change, it allows us to adapt sooner and more productively the next time. Even when mistakes happen along the road, those mistakes come from the courage of taking a step. Every time you take that one small step, you are stepping further away from the fear.

There are many ways in the world to be successful. But most people think of celebrities, artist, politicians, and businessmen whenever they heard the word success.

Moreover, they think doing what they will make you successful but that not the case. They forget the most basic thing that makes a person successful that is their hard work, dedication, and the desire to achieve their dream. More importantly, they what they like to do not what that others told them to do. Successful people do what they like to do also they do what they feel correct for their business.

What is the harm of success?

We all knew that we can't achieve something without sacrificing something. Success also demands various things from you. But these sacrifices will not go in vain if you achieve your goal.

Certainly, many people achieve professional success but in doing so they fail in achieving mental, social and physical success. The tension of lacking behind in other things pulls them apart.

Also, there are cases where people became so obsessed with success that the people around them start to feel uncomfortable around them. In some cases, they have gone mad. Apart from that, people also get depressed if they can't achieve success like others. So, we can say that there is much harm to success.

Success and hard work

It may sound unfit to some peoples but success depends a lot of hard work. Without it, you can't become successful. Hard work does not mean that you do laborious work or the work that make you sweat. Hard work means having a healthy body, strong mind, willpower and positive attitude towards things. And for all those things you need energy. So, be attentive to your body and soul.

Besides, do not just work on your program, push your limit, take charge of other things, improve your skills and most importantly keep learning. Apart from that, be with positive peoples, develop positive habits, and do exercise not only for the body but also for your mind.

What is a success? How is it defined? It can be defined as achievement of your goals or even having small occasions where you feel to have achieved something. Whatever it is, it surely brings a smile to your face and brings happiness in your life. But even a robber feel it a success on committing as successful robbery. Can it be termed as a success?

What is a success? How is it defined? It can be defined as achievement of your goals or even having small occasions where you feel to have achieved something. Whatever it is, it surely brings a smile to your face and brings happiness in your life. But even a robber feel it a success on committing as successful robbery. Can it be termed as a success?

None can deny that the world blindly respects and trusts wealthy people. Money is the prime dynamic force that drives this world. The sooner we acknowledge and appreciate this fact the better. Academic success is a prime concern for all in the initial part of life, especially in the school days. For those who continue perusing studies, academic success is the epitome of everything. It is mostly observed that success in personal life becomes a tough task for those who have all the riches. Here is where the common people feel successful to have a happy personal life.

One should not regret their decisions taken in the past and must refrain dwelling in the past. We must give deep thought before taking any decisions and uttering words from the mouth. For making a successful decision one must ask questions to oneself like: What Do I Need To Do? What Will Be The Outcome? Will It Be Worth Doing? One must keep the emotions for success and failures intact and should not showcase it to others. Successful people never wait for applause or acknowledgement of their work as they eventually get it. To become successful one must keep friends close and enemies closer. A successful person never demeans the weak and never underestimates anyone.

To become successful one has to understand what is important in that instant, recognize and work on the weaknesses, take criticism and hold on to the strengths. From a broader perspective Success defines the contentment, peace of mind and sheer happiness that is achieved. One should remember that only perseverance can lead the path to success.

Real success is something we should all strive to attain. Real success can simply be said to be achieving a higher position or very high position in our chosen field or area; it can be politics or business or even education. In the world we live in today, we have equated success to riches, prosperity, fortunes, cars, houses and so many mundane things. We believe that once a person has enough money to be able to afford what he or she wants, the person is successful.

Success is much more than riches, power or fame. Success is simply the feeling of satisfaction and happiness one gets from leading a particular way of life or carrying out a particular activity. Success in any field or aspect of life can only be achieved through serious hard work and a little bit of opportunity. One of the most important recipes of success is determination and it might as well be the most important secret of success. To become successful, it is necessary to never give up until the aim of happiness and satisfaction in life is fully met. The happiness and satisfaction can be found in very different things in different people.

'Success' is a very powerful word. Many of us run behind it; most of us want to conquer it. So, what is success all about? Does this mean acquiring money or fame? Success means different things to different people.

Definition of Success

The Oxford dictionary defines success as "The accomplishment of an aim or purpose".

This is the definition of success in theory, but in reality it differs according to people's interests and goals.

It is very important for every individual to define their own concept of success rather than following someone else's footsteps. We must analyze what makes us happy, what gives us contentment, and what motivates us. No one can list out our needs better than us.

True success means understanding our dreams and working joyfully to make those dreams come true.

How to Achieve Success

Many great people have suggested various ways to achieve success. But the real secret ingredient to nail success is to believe that we are already successful. With this strong affirmative thought, success can be easily achieved if we follow these three success factors:-

We should follow our passion because that is where our heart and soul is. When we follow our passion there is no need for us to put any extra effort.

The path to success is always challenging. We should build confidence to face any challenging situations.

The third and most important success factor is discipline. When we work in a disciplined manner, things will automatically fall in place.

If we stick to these three factors, nothing can stop us from tasting success. Success is a journey which continues even after the goal is achieved.

Success is perhaps the most desired feeling that all of us want to experience in the pursuit of our goals and also in day to day life. Apparently, every individual has his or her own definition of success.

Parameters of Success

None can deny that the world blindly respects and trusts wealthy people. Money is the prime dynamic force that drives this world. The sooner we acknowledge and appreciate this fact the better. Academic success is a prime concern for all in the initial part of life, especially in the school days. For those who continue perusing studies, academic success is the epitome of everything. It is mostly observed that success in personal life becomes a tough task for those who have all the riches. Here is where the common people feel successful to have a happy personal life.

Qualities for Achieving Success

One should not regret their decisions taken in the past and must refrain dwelling in the past. We must give deep thought before taking any decisions and uttering words from the mouth. For making a successful decision one must ask questions to oneself like: What Do I Need To Do? What Will Be The Outcome? Will It Be Worth Doing? One must keep the emotions for success and failures intact and should not showcase it to others. Successful people never wait for applause or acknowledgement of their work as they eventually get it. To become successful one must keep friends close and enemies closer. A successful person never demeans the weak and never underestimates anyone.

To become successful one has to understand what is important in that instant, recognize and work on the weaknesses, take criticism and hold on to the strengths. From a broader perspective Success defines the contentment, peace of mind and sheer happiness that is achieved. One should remember that only perseverance can lead the path to success.

Real success is something we should all strive to attain. Real success can simply be said to be achieving a higher position or very high position in our chosen field or area; it can be politics or business or even education. In the world we live in today, we have equated success to riches, prosperity, fortunes, cars, houses and so many mundane things. We believe that once a person has enough money to be able to afford what he or she wants, the person is successful. This is a total and complete misconception that will be discussed here.

Money isn't a measure of success?

While it is important to note that having money is a part of being successful and you can classify as rich person as being successful, money is not all that success is about and we have a lot of people around us that are seemingly rich but still count themselves as not successful. In fact, sometimes we see wealthy people and conclude that they aren't successful. If this is true then we can safely conclude that success is deeper that money or other superficial and physical things can we might acquire or own. Money is very important to success in life but it is not a necessity and neither is it the only key to success in life.

Real success is way beyond the physical things we can see, real success is all about the feeling of satisfaction we get when we accomplish a task or do something, it is the happiness we get just by remembering what we have achieved and how we did it, real success has to do with a lot of positive feelings about ourselves and pride in what we have been able to do. As we can see, real success can only be achieved within one's self and that is why a lot of people who we think are successful still believe they aren't just because they aren't happy with what they are doing or they feel they can get so much more out of life. From this, we can see that it is very important to attain true success in life.

For one to be successful, the first and most important thing one needs to do is to set goals and objectives. Only through the setting of goals can one really have something to pursue and claim success when we got those things or meet the set goals and target. A very important ingredient in achieving real success is determination. If one is going to get real success, one has to be determined to never give up no matter what the situation might be. Another very important ingredient is hard work as we can't expect to be successful if we don't work hard and do all it takes to meet all of our set goals. It is important that we get all the skills that are required for us to be successful in our chosen field.

You can inspire yourself by being a self-motivator and critic. It opens room for self-improvement and appreciation. As it is said that 'well begun is half done,' do not hesitate to sparkle a start. Once we get a push, the rest will fall right in place. Even if we stumble down a couple of times, do not let go of our dreams. Failures are part and parcel of any successful entity. Mistakes are quite common and what needs to do is that we acknowledge them, and bear them in our mind. It ensures that we learn from the mistakes and in turn do not repeat them.

Nobody has ever been successful overnight. Patience is yet another golden rule. Just convince your mind that you are strong enough to be successful, though not today, at least some day. Never be disappointed if you lose. Trust in yourself and believe that you will reach there and you deserve to reach there. Your strength and weakness define the person you are, and the realization of it is rather important. Selfless dedication and hard work will definitely get you there.

Once you achieve your goals, you can be a strong inspiration to others. There is a warrior in you and never shut it down. You are capable of climbing higher and boom into a fantastic personality. Whatsoever, live a humble life, spread positivity and bear the torch to others' road to success.

rather saying education is the road to success is just another way of saying education is very important for all of us in life, without education there would not be a lot of progression in both our individual and collective lives as human. It is very important that we get education in order to get success in life. Most times, people generally limit education to the four walls of a classroom or a school.

Education has roots in every area of our existence; education can be said to begin from the home, parents and family members educate and train the children on good characters that they should imbibe and teach them to remove some habits and characters. All of these good characters imbibed by the child through education at home can help the child become very successful in future.

We all know that without good characters and morals, it is extremely hard to become successful or make it in life as people would not want to be associated with such person. We are also educated on good communication and interpersonal skills that are very necessary for us to make it and become successful in life.

importance of education in success=

We need to know the true value and worth of education. Education helps to facilitate our skill, knowledge and learning; it gives us a different view of the world and refines our personality, helping us to build very positive attitudes. Education is a totally essential tool in ensuring a bright future.

Education can go a very long way in changing our thoughts and level of reasoning; it broadens our worldview and provides us with the opportunity to get knowledge and technical skills that are highly needed in life. We can improve our knowledge level and skill by watching educational documentaries and programmes on the TV, reading the news and keeping up to date with all of the happenings all over the world, reading a lot of books that can educate us. Education can go a long way to make us into more rational and civilised people. Education guarantees our place among people in the society and can help us achieve all of our dreams and aspirations in life.

Education and success

Success is the goal of all of us and it is our mission. Life can sometimes be full of different opportunities and challenges. Success can only be attained if we have all of the required and needed tools.

The most important tool for success is education because without education, we wouldn't be able to have a wide view of the world and be able to innovate and develop. A lot of youths and children today cite the examples of the successful people that didn't graduate from school and still went ahead to be successful in life. Mark Zuckerberg, the founder of Facebook famously did not graduate from Harvard university but still went ahead to become very successful. The truth is even though Mark didn't graduate, he was well educated and wouldn't have been able to start Facebook if he had no knowledge of coding and wasn't enrolled in Harvard at all. From him, we can learn that education isn't limited and can basically be any way of widening our knowledge and improving ourselves. We should never confuse education with getting a diploma or a degree. Only education in or out of school can make us be successful in life and give us the true career we want.

if you've been feeling a little low lately, this essay on success is sure to boost your motivation levels and set the goals right for you! We hear about so many successful people from all the areas. Some of them may be our favorite singers, actors, scientists, writers, social workers, politicians, and what not. Their achievements inspire the hearts of many and urge them to do better.While we tend to focus on the sensation of the final outcome, the journey toward the goal is what matters the most. Sadly, human nature forces us to look at everything through the eyes of instant gratification. But the stories of success are not created overnight. In real life, any small big achievement demands tons of efforts and sacrifices.

If success is a building, consider each effort to be a brick, that has to be put in day and night tirelessly. Dreaming about achieving a goal in life is a lovely idea. Nonetheless, working on it every day is more than just a fantasy. You have to make it happen.Do you pray or meditate? What happens at that moment? You sit quietly and focus all your attention and energy into the prayer or in watching those thoughts. Prayer commands sincerity. True worshipping is when the heart is pure and honest.

In the same way, success is a conscientious phenomenon. It asks for dedication and ethical diligence. For a real success, there are no shortcuts and there is no quitting too! Yes, we all get tired and hopeless. That doesn't mean we have to give in to those feelings and quit. Keep working no matter what!At times, when you feel that you can't go on anymore, take a break. Rejuvenate yourself, talk to your loved ones, rest a lot, create a fresh perspective. And come back again with a greater force and zeal. You never know when the efforts will turn into the sweet fruits of success. One thing common in all the great personalities was that they never quit!

A prosperous life is not strictly about having all the materialistic comforts around. To some extent, this may be true. But, all in all, it's only a microscopic way to measure someone's success.

Everybody's favorite, the great feminist and poetess, Maya Angelou says, "Success is liking yourself, liking what you do, and liking how you do it."Winston Churchill quotes it as, "Success is stumbling from failure to failure with no loss of enthusiasm."Not to mention, America's former first lady, Michelle Obama who expresses her own views on success. According to her, "Success isn't about how much money you make. It's about the difference you make in people's lives."In the words of Albert Einstein, "Strive not to be a success, but rather to be of value."Anne Sweeney, who remained the president of the Disney Channel from 1996 to 2014. In her words, "Define success on your own terms, achieve it by your own rules, and build a life you're proud to live."It is evident enough how these miraculous and charismatic visionaries have described success in various terms and that there is no particular way to define it. The only authentic parameter should be your own satisfaction and happiness.

FAILURES ARE THE PILLARS TO SUCCESS

We have understood that success is an abstract notion. Now, it is time to get to the bottom and explore some basic questions about it. Have you ever tried to inquire into what success means to you? What are the things that would make you convinced that you are a successful person now? Does your heart yearn for fame, money, peace, joy, love, or something else?These questions are crucial. They make your mind clear and set your priorities more effectively. Always remember that a virtue that appeals to you may not mean the same to another person. Everybody has their own preferences and goals in life.The bottom line is regardless of what the goal is, we can each be successful in our lives as long as the achievement makes us happy and content. It could be your education, a well-paying job, having a loving family, social security, or freedom to live the way you want to.Anything, no matter how small or big, that fills us with a sense of purpose and gratifies the heart leads to success. If you are a happy person and love your life, then success is yours! For a long time, our minds have been trained to believe that money is the greatest source of joy. However, it's not true!Undoubtedly, wealth is a strong means to create comfort and security for us. But if it was the only thing needed for success, why do the richest people still deal with depression, anxiety, fears, and failures? Have you ever thought about it?

Physical wealth does not guarantee an insusceptibility to dissatisfaction and failure. Thinking otherwise would only create a bottomless void within you. People madly run after money and career. And yet when they are well-established, they still may not feel the joy and peace within. What is the missing piece in their lives?

Success in LifeLife is a rollercoaster, isn't it! We all have our own strengths and weaknesses. Overcoming your flaws and frailty is a victory in itself. If you are thinking of coming out as a winner in life, don't confine yourself to monetary values.

With money, you may feel "technically" rich and yet have no access to the truest joy.There are many dimensions to success. But everything depends upon our ability to recognize them. What are these dimensions, by the way! Let us explore a few of them.You must have heard the famous quote, "Health is Wealth". We need to understand the hidden value of this quote today more than ever. Ask yourself, if you would be able to enjoy anything in the same way if you were suffering from an acute or chronic illness? No, but such physical ailments are a bitter truth to many. To these people, achieving a partial or full recovery, having a long and respectful life is a success.For the emotional souls, having their loved ones around, giving them a quality life, and taking care of them is what counts as the real victory. A person who cares about the whole society, for him/ her the true meaning of succeeding would be providing the basic amenities to the underprivileged, fighting for human rights, or creating awareness.And yes, the biggest of the aims could be as simple and meaningful as leading a peaceful life. It could be about not having regrets and ill feelings toward others. They could also be as big as winning a gold medal in the Olympics, breaking the stereotypes, getting out of a toxic relationship and having a stable life.The point is, success cannot be put into a singular category. And comparing one's goal with the other person would be like comparing apple to an orange, or fruits to vegetables. Each person is unique. Their journey of life is different and so are their goals and parameters of success.

Success for Students

The keys to successful academic life are open secrets. As a student, your progress depends on the level of self-discipline, dedication, and hard work. If you are able to pull off these habits in long-term success would never leave you. Right? Nonetheless, the matter is not so simple.In today's time, students are looking for "success" more desperately than ever!

Considering the cut-throat competitions, it is quite understandable also. The pressure of family's expectations makes things even more complicated. The students have no option except to excel in their studies, but at what costs?First of all, academic success is dependent on a limited number of subjects. The true potential of a child or a young one cannot be fairly measured based on such a narrow line. Moreover, somehow we have come to believe that excellent grades are a must for a student's survival in this world. Fortunately, that's not completely correct.The practical life is much more than a few subjects. Most of the things we learn at school and colleges are plain theories. The bookish knowledge hardly proves to be of any help in the real world. What makes you rich is the experiences you gain on a daily basis.Of course, this doesn't mean that grades and books shouldn't be taken seriously at all. You need to understand that these things play a partial role in forming the ladder of success. The better word to focus on would be 'growth'.If winning the race and grabbing a seat in some reputed college takes a toll on your mental, physical, and psychological health, then, we are seriously doing something wrong here. After all, these are the same factors leading to the rising number of suicides among the youths.Not getting good marks doesn't mean that you are not good enough for anything. It just means that you haven't explored everything yet. There are many great personalities like Einstein, Leonardo da Vinci, J.K. Rowling, who were a failure on the scales of conventional methods. But they proved everyone wrong.All you need to remember is that never lose faith in yourself. If you really love what you do and consistently pour all of your energy into that task, then, definitely success is waiting for you! Make a routine of your choice and follow it religiously. Stay punctual. Fix your eyes on the goal and keep working.

Success and Hard Work

You can only work hard when you are fit overall. A good health is not just about having a strong body but also a strong mind and willpower. For all these things, you need energy. So, pay attention to things that you are feeding to your sensory organs. This includes from the proper diet to releasing stress, stay positive, working out, having those around who believe in you.Don't just work hard on your curriculum only. Take charge of other aspects too. As much as possible, include healthy foods in the diet. Staying positive induces good hormones in the body and the effect clearly shows in your performance. To strengthen your mental health, meditate every day.Sitting around greenery, talking to your loved ones, reading positive books, are some of the other ways to replenish your energy levels. Make sure to work out every day, or at least go for a 30-minutes walk. Keep yourself hydrated. Drink plenty of water and other fluids.Apart from focusing on the positive steps, be careful of the negative factors too. For instance, any negative conversation or toxic people in your life may suck away all your energy and charm. Try your best to avoid these triggers. Not only that, distractions like television, online chats, social media, parties, etc. should not be underestimated.Keep your body and mind clean like a temple. It will help you work harder and with more effectiveness. There are no shortcuts to success. However, prefer to work smart rather than work hard. Never ever neglect the amount of sleep you get. There is no substitute for proper sleep.Lack of sleep makes you cranky. Your concentration and memory become poorer. The learning becomes slower. So, a million dollar advice would be to get sufficient sleep, that means up to 8-10 hours. A few hours may be up and down depending on the person's body requirements.

It is okay if the hard work makes you tired. However, the whole idea of hard work should not suffocate you. They say that if you love what you do, you don't have to work a day in your life! If the set goals don't well-align with your heart, explore something that does. Your goals should be set by you and not anyone else.

Success and Failure

Do you fear failure? What is the definition of failure according to you? How important is a failure for success? Let us find some answers to these amazing questions and doubts that we all face within us. To make things easier, here are a few great quotes for you!"Only those who dare to fail greatly can ever achieve greatly." – Robert F. Kennedy"Giving up is the only sure way to fail." – Gena Showalter"I have not failed. I've just found 10,000 ways that won't work." – Thomas A. EdisonMust have changed your perspective a bit! Well, it won't be wrong to say that failure is a part of success. It is an inevitable part of that process. Like two sides of a coin. You cannot expect to taste success until you have learned to embrace the failures.

There is an interesting story about it with a strong message. There used to live a guy who owned a grand and luxurious car. That car always stayed inside the house. The man never drove it. One day, one of his friends visited him and asked the reason for not taking the car out on the road.Do you know what the man replied? He said that he would take the car out when all the traffic lights are green. He was waiting for an impossible thing to happen! Can you believe that? It's ironic but yes, we all do the same metaphorically.When we don't take steps due to the fear of failure, subconsciously, we are waiting for everything to be perfect. So perfect that there would be no tiny scope for failing. That means there would be no red lights at all. How is that even possible!

Leave the fear of failure behind. The only thing you should be scared of is not making efforts. Because that kills even the slightest chance of success. Be humble and embrace failure. Learn from your mistakes. These lessons are valuable. No book would teach you the way your experiences will.Success is a cumulative and relative term. Without peace and love, money and fame don't count as success. True success would satiate your soul. It would fill your life with joy. Shrug off the idea of comparing your life with someone else's. Every person follows a different path and journey. That is why the meaning of success also varies from one individual to another.No matter how difficult or impossible seems the goal, never quit. Keep working and one day you would succeed. Don't confine your ambitions to just making money. Listen to your heart and follow it. The voices within us are our guiding lights!

Regardless of culture, race, religion, economic background or social group, most would agree that success is important and vital to the well-being of the individual, the family unit, the group and certainly to the survival of those things into the future. Those that minimize the importance of success are either confused or have given up on their own chances of success.
Success provides confidence, security, a sense of well-being, the ability to contribute at a greater level, hope and leadership. Without success, you, the group, your company, your goals, dreams and even entire civilizations cease to survive. Without continued success, the company, dream, even entire races will cease to exist, as was the case with the Vikings, Romans, Greeks, American Indians and then an endless list of companies and products. Success is important in that it is required in order to continue on!

Success should never be reduced to something that does not matter or isn't important. It is vital and should be held as such! If you are unable to succeed in taking care of your children, they will be taken over by the state. For an individual or group to continue on, he or she must actively accomplish his or her goals and targets (succeed) or he or she will cease to exist. For a business or industry to continue on, it must be successful in creating new products, getting those products to the market, keeping clients, employees and investors happy and repeating that cycle, over and over.

Cute sayings that somehow dismiss the importance of success abound, like, "Success is a journey, not a destination." Please! When your future viability is threatened, these cute little sayings will prove to be poor substitution for success. The last couple of years of economic turmoil should have made it obvious that we all underestimated how much success is needed and how valuable it actually is to our survival and well-being.Regardless of what goals you are trying to attain, success is important. Quit succeeding, and you quit winning; quit winning long enough, and you will quit! Do your kids benefit when they see mom and daddy losing? Does anyone benefit when you can't get your art sold, or you can't get that great book published, or you have some great idea that will improve the world, but can't succeed in bringing it to the world?

I wanted to tell you a story about a mason jar and change. That may sound really strange, but those two things really do go together. Did you ever do something that you thought was mundane and other people thought was profound? Did you downplay how amazing you were? Brushing off the little things that we do to propel forward is not stressing the importance of success. Every success. Even the little ones.One of the big reasons that I needed this jar was because I had this silly notion in my head that everything I know, everyone else already knows. That is downplaying my success (obtaining the knowledge) and not counting them as a successes.

I honestly used to think that the phrase, "Some people don't succeed because they are afraid of success", was stupid. I couldn't figure out why ANYONE would be afraid of what they want the most. Unfortunately, there is truth to it. Being successful is scary. The more you downplay what you know, the less you are going forward because you think that you are just another person doing the same thing as everyone else.I needed a swift kick in the head to get rid of that. You are successful and do successful things each day. Do you give yourself credit?

I don't care if you got your to-do list done and that was all you can think of to write down. Guess what? Most people NEVER get it done, so you are ahead of the pack.Here is proof of my jar: (I have a crafting addiction so I had PLENTY of foam and glue and ribbon to make this on hand. Oh, and glitter, of course!)If you are not a crafty person, that's OK. Someone else in your house can make it, or you just get some tape and write "Success Jar" on it. I don't care, but get it done. This can really help propel you forward by realizing that everything you do is important.When you look back at the end of the week, you will be able to see how far you have come. (Note: The day of the week that you read the jar should be the same every week. I started on a Wednesday, but I want to open on Mondays, so I'm going to have a few extra the first time. Put it on your to-do list as an action item to read them!Are you ready to make your jar? I want to see pictures so please post them on social media and tag me so I can see them. I want to celebrate with you!

XIII

For students
IMPORTANT POINTS

"Consistency is more important than perfection". Being consistent with the work makes you perfect and then perfections are ultimately enhanced in a person. Consistency is a key to success ,when you are doing the work with consistency definitely it will be perfect.

I would like to share the real story of M.S. Dhoni. During the trailer launch of M.S. Dhoni biopic in 2016, a student asked dhoni about the ways that could help him maintain composture in stressful situation like exams. He replied that he learnt a life lesson from his dad long back when he asked for his permission to play cricket during his board exams.

So , his father replied in that situation.

He said, "if you have studied for whole year , then one day wont make a difference and if you haven't studied for whole year then also one day wont make difference"

What we understood from this story that consistency is the most fundamental virtue to ahieve our dreams .

When a person is consistent , they do the same thing over and over, they do the same process until it produces a desired result. Consistency can decrease the amount of time we are unprepared for the curve balls life throws at us. If you are passionate and determined to clear your goal then be consistent to your preparation that you are doing to achieve your goal don't stop it.

Another important thing is to give 100 % without excepting 100% in return. Dhoni further said that his passion was cricket and whenever he played cricket he played with 100% intensity and commitment but he never worried whether he would get selected in the Indian cricket team or not. Similarly, when we talk about goals we should not be so worried about it much about the outcomes and the failures instead give your 100% in that. We should enjoy the journey rather than worrying too much about destination.

"Success isn't about greatness. Its about consistency. Consistent hard work leads to success."

Being consistent means dedicating your self to your goals and staying focused on things and activities to achieve your goals.

According to Ryan Rios and Mark Atalla , consistency in your efforts leads to self- discipline, teaches your self control, improve your overall personality and builds momentum.

Consistency at work often leads to higher productivity, so you may finish more tasks throughout your work day , because of your increased productivity, management may trust you to contribute to a higher number of projects or have more responsibilities.

"Success doesn't come from what you do occasionally, it comes from what you do consistently."

-MARIE FORLE

No matter how hard you try to be consistent, you are going to make mistakes from time to time. Therefore, try to keep going even if you make a mistake. Even if you are incredibly organized, you are going to slip up from time to time. Therefore, you should plan from mistakes along the way. If you make a mistake, try not to beat yourself up for it. This is something that happens from time to time. Even if you break a promise, miss a deadline, or have to cancel on somebody, this doesn't necessarily mean you are ruining your consistency.

Another important have it you need to develop if you would like to be more consistent is to only make promises you can actually keep. People like to be liked by other people. Therefore, we all have a tendency to say yes when someone asks us for help. Even though it is good to help us other than we can, it is important not to make

"Opportunities are like sunrise .If you wait too long , you miss them."

-William Ward

Opportunities are key to success , as you unlock the door of success with key of opportunities ultimately many opportunities will start blossoming.

Opportunities will not come for you , you need to create it. "humans are created but you can recreate yourself."

If we get the opportunity we should not leave it.

"The pessimist sees difficulty in every opportunity. the optimist sees opportunity in every difficulty."

-Winston Churchill

I would like to tell here the story of leaving the opportunities which come to you so,A fellow was stuck on his rooftop in a flood. He was praying to God for help. The stranded fellow shouted back, "No, it's OK, I'm praying to God and he is going to save me."

So the rowboat went on.

Then a motorboat came by. "The fellow in the motorboat shouted, "Jump in, I can save you."

To this the stranded man said, "No thanks, I'm praying to God and he is going to save me. I have faith."

So the motorboat went on.

Then a helicopter came by and the pilot shouted down, "Grab this rope and I will lift you to safety."

To this the stranded man again replied, "No thanks, I'm praying to God and he is going to save me. I have faith."

So the helicopter reluctantly flew away.

Soon the water rose above the rooftop and the man drowned. He went to Heaven. He finally got his chance to discuss this whole situation with God, at which point he exclaimed, "I had faith in you but you didn't save me, you let me drown. I don't understand why!"

To this God replied, "I sent you a rowboat and a motorboat and a helicopter, what more did you expect?"

I will give you 4 tips that can give you opportunities .

1. Think of How Everything Can be Improved

Some of the greatest opportunities are not mind-blowing new inventions; they are mostly iterative improvements to existing things. Consider the Dyson Vacuum Cleaner. Vacuum cleaners already existed. Still, Sir James Dyson figured he could improve the design by removing the annoyance of having to constantly buy and replace the bag. On this simple iterative improvement, he built the Dyson empire that disrupted an industry. Sir James went on to do it again by creating the first useable cordless Dyson Vacuum cleaner. An improvement on an already existing invention. I own one, it was exorbitantly expensive, but now we can clean the entire house in 10 minutes, instead of hours.

Everything can be improved; the key is to find things that you can improve. The next time you are annoyed by a product or service, think about what you would do to improve it.

2. What Do You Do Better Than Most?

We are all good at something. Think about what you are good at, usually what you excel at is something you enjoy. For some, it is writing, graphic design, or coding.

Head on over to Up works to see what thousands of people are doing to unlock opportunities and earn money doing the things they love.

Mostly the peoples do very interestingly things that they like and it creates opportunity for them in that situation.

3. People Love To Talk: Listen & Learn

It is so easy to fall into the trap of talking about yourself. I personally have an internal alarm bell that sounds when I realize that I have been the only one talking for the last 10 minutes. Don't be the mindless talker, be the listener. Start conversations, ask questions, engage, but when you find yourself rambling on, be aware it is time to let others express themselves. I certainly have learned a lot from simply listening to people. Also, by listening, truly listening, and understanding, you can get the measure of a person.

4. Be Trustworthy – Always

Honour, respect, and trust are three things you should live by. You should never betray the trust of others unless, of course, they are an murdering serial killer, then it's OK. Being seen as trustworthy unlocks so many potential opportunities, be they friendships, partnerships, or insights. Being the rock means you have the respect of others, and they will want to help and promote you without you even having to ask.

"Never give up because great things take time."

I would like to share my personal experience . Once everyone were busy in their work no one was talking with me as I thought that I am very alone no one is there for me . I became very sad with situation and then fully I had lose my hopes . Then my best friend told me , "You only lose the hope when you quit trying."

Then I felt the spark of determination burn in my blood. I wont quit the situation and will not give up.

Then from that day I was never alone and started writing different poems and stories they were with me.

"Never give up today because you never know what tomorrow may bring."

Again I would share a story of the person who discovered the submarine that was john holyand he was poor and he would get the money only sufficient to live as he was a teacher . we wanted to discover a submarine.

Then he made a small submarine with poor quality engine so it cant float on water then everyone started saying him mad even his father saying him mad .

Then John got to know that no one cares for him hear so he went to America. There some journalist came to meet him then they also said him mad . so all were saying that mad person of inside came outside.

Now everywhere he go everyone started insulting him .

Walking on road for him became difficult for him, but he got a opportunity from peoples of Ireland to make submarine then they gav 2 lakhs fifty thousand to john and he started making that submarine everyone knew that now the submarine which will be made will be definetly success full. But that time in that team of Ireland everyone became enmy of each other and some of that members took submarine and hide on a certain place , this situation brought stress on john due to submarine which was hidden because other team members were asking for it.

Then after that the minister of that America odered that from country the sketch of that submarine should be send to court then many sketches of that submarine were there but the best one was of john again he got one more opportunity then he was given some engineers for his support . but asthe engineers were more intelligent then him and have studied more.

So they showed there potential on john .In this situation john fell ill and then he was absent for some period of time in that project .

The engineers took the advantage of the situation and they did the submarine as per them so the submarine which was created became very waste as it was not in good condition .

Now everyone were blaming to john but john after facing this didn't gave up and he proved that it was just because of engineers disturbance.

So from this story we got that john after facing such difficulties in his life he still didn't gave up and after that he reated his own company to graete submarines and many engineers visited him and they buyed the sketch of submarine.

Life is full of ups and downs. Everything can change in a matter of seconds and we can't do anything about it. All we can do is feel sorry for the effort and the time lost in pursuing life. That's what those think who believe we are slaves to our destiny. The reality is we make our destiny. We decide our fate.

Often, it becomes easy to just give up on our dreams for good because they are costing us a lot in lost comfort, money, time, and so on. The fact is that all these "expenses incurred" are investments. When we believe in ourselves, we do not get afraid of failures. Every fall, we get back up and never even think about giving up. Contrarily, those who are already afraid of the unknown, find temporary failures to be an excuse to pack up.

Apart from the ultimate success, a positive attitude makes the journey all the more interesting. We learn new things each day and make more sense of the world around us. We come to know that fantasies are there for a reason. It is because we can turn them into reality through persistence and perseverance.

There comes that second in the entirety of our lives when we feel like totally giving up when nothing appears to go the manner in which we arranged, and the future looks depressing, best case scenario. On occasions such as these, we can't resist the opportunity to feel that there can't be motivated to continue to attempt; all things considered, why in dealing with something when you realize it will be purposeless eventually? However, to be reasonable, it is never a smart thought to simply give up, not until you have given your best into the circumstance.

One point that each person should keep in his/her brain is that no one in this whole world is awesome and nobody could at any point be. Everybody commits errors, and it isn't the missteps that exacerbate you than others; it is your conduct after those slip-ups. Assuming you right those slip-ups and accomplish your objective, you are the saint, and in the event that you abandon your fantasies only for a misstep that you made, then, at that point, you never had any objective or dream on which you were working in any case.

There was once a rich man who, every night before going to sleep, prayed the same prayer to his God. In his prayer, he would say, "God, please do this one favour for me, at least this one. I have been asking you for this my whole life. Everyone knows that I am the most unhappy man on earth. Why have you made my life full of problems? I am ready to exchange my problems with anybody else, anybody will do. I'm not asking to live my life without problems, I just can't deal with these no more. It is unfair that I have such big problems to solve, and so many of them, while others have such easy ones and only a few. Can't you give me only this single opportunity to exchange all of my problems with somebody else? I believe I am not asking for too much!"And finally, one night, while everyone in the town including the rich man were asleep God appeared in all of their dreams at once and gave the following instructions, "Gather all of your miseries and big problems into one bag and bring the bag to the temple hall." At first, no one believed what has happened. But slowly everyone's mindset shifted from this is not possible too "what if it's true." Soon everyone in town started packing their problems into the biggest bag they could find and carried them to the temple hall.

The rich man was so happy that this day had finally come. He rushed with filling his bag and started to walk towards the hall with the biggest smile he had for a long time. While walking towards the temple hall he noticed that everyone else in his town was either filling a bag or already had a full bag and was walking towards the temple. He was a bit surprised that everyone else thought they had big problems worth exchanging too. By the time he reaches the hall, he became very afraid, because he saw people are carrying bigger bags than he was. And these were the people that he had always seen smiling in beautiful clothes and always saying nice things to each other.

The rich man slowly became a little hesitant about whether to or not to go and exchange the bag. But then again he has been praying for his whole life for this opportunity so he decided to continue and see what happens. When he enters the hall he heard a voice saying to put his bag down in the center as everyone else did. And when he did so he heard the voice again, but this time the voice told him to take a look around and to choose one bag. But once he would pick the new bag there would be no turning back. Everyone stood still and carefully looked around to inspect the size of other bags.

And then a miracle happened. Instead of taking a different bag, everyone rushed to their own. Without thinking too much the rich man also rushes towards his own bag, afraid that somebody else would take it. To his own surprise, he didn't take advantage of his wish that came true. When walking back home he thought why he reacted the way he did. And the answer surprised him. The truth was that his big problems weren't actually that big, and he actually knew how to deal with them. While on the other hand, he didn't have the slightest clue how to deal with the problems of other people.

So there fore, Your mindset is very important. If you focus on the bad, that is what you will find. But if you focus on the good you will find it.

Having mindset is very important because if you wanted to do anything that also with a target that you have to fullfill that at any cost then you have a mindset for it .

Now just imagine that you wanted to become a IAS officer so just you said once that you wanted to be IAS officer then you have to have a mindset for it .

Working on that mindset is also very important . what is the meaning of that word mindset it means that your mind is set for doing the task that your mind suggests and it is also very helpful to achieve success.

My final exam has there of grade 7th and I didn't went to school for 3 months and I was also unaware about the topics that are going to come in exam before five to six days of exam I got the syllabus and then I had set my mind hat whatever may happen I have to score good in exam above 95% then after settting my mind I got up to study and was ready .

For that exam period I didn't played , didn't watch T.v. , didn't watch social media etc.. then I was with that moto that I have to score then anything may come in between I will not stop .

After I set mind I don't know what happened to me that I was very busy in my studies and didn't even thought that I can complete the whole portion with completions of notebook but you know when you set your mind tha yes you have to do it then whatever may happen you will do it but yes mindset doesn't mean that just once saying that I want to do this . All is of your effort you have to do .

Your mind will do anything for you but you must have that confidence and never changing goal and work for it. Actually you have to work for it more than you hope for it. So stop hoping for it because nothing will happen due to yours hoping you have to work for it.

You can set your mind and work for it to but yes one thing keep in mind that whatever you do before doing that ask to yourself that really can you do it so should start but if answer comes no then stop there only because when you will go ahead in your journey and then you think to take turn then you have to work for your other goal from first.

So to avoid this first only begin with goal that can be fulfilled.

Everything is in your hand from thinking to making it reality but you have to decide that you just want to think about your dreams and be on the place where you are or you have to go ahead .

Your mind works 24 hours for you but where to utilise that working of mind also depends upon you on the things that will give you back no result or on the things that will give you result. Its just like you are caught by fire and at that movement you are thinking how the fire caught instead you should act to save your self.I have noticed the peoplewho make very good timetables of the day to be followed but unfortunetly they are not successfully followed so for that you haesto set a goal for the day instead of locking yourself in that timetable .

Way that will help you do the work for your day. Instead of making whole timetable of month so definetly who it will be possible follow that sometimes some evets can come or there may be any fuction so the timetable may not be followed so what you have to do is just make to do list as you sit for study and then after making that to do list follow those tasks of particular day

No need to give any time slots that you have to do that thing at that time only because it can happen some work may take more time or some may take less but have a clear mindset to complete that task.

"Kick your goals before goals kick you."

If you want success with your goals it's very essential that you goal should be focused by you ,you should not be distracted from your goal.

In fact ,we face many and more obstacles in path of achieving success but the key to success is focus on goals not on the obstacles.

But yes the question comes how to focus on our dreams and goals? So answer to this questION

Keep reminding yourself of big picture, no matter what it , there is always going to be something we don't like.

"Having the big pictures in mind enables us to overcome the day to day routines that attempt to distract us from pursuing our dreams."

-**Assegid Habtewold.**

Some tasks comes that make us lose our patience and focus. During the task that make you feel like this, you have to think if you can do anything to change it.

If no, then remind your self to the big picture. Remind yourself that every

Little thing adds up to your efforts to fullfill your dreams.

"If you spend your life over analyzing every encounter you will always see the tree, but never the forest."

Next is, remind yourself reason why you started if you knew the reason that why you started then one thing will be confirmed that if you started then you need to finish it. It is just like a race which you have participated but just participation is not only important the thing that is more important that is you gave to win it .

So think of ending that race with your efforts and you need to struggle for it.

"if you can perceive it, your mind can believe it, only then you can achieve it."

To realize your dreams, the dreams must be realistic. Keeping in mind once interest and strengths and limitation too. I would like highlight the difference between your goals and dreams.

Dreams are just desires or wishes. Desires are probably weak because they don't have directions or deadlines that is what difference of

dreams from goals. Goals are the dreams with deadlines and an action plan.

So actually what is important is not to have the big dreams but to have well defined goals to realize the dreams.

We have to set up goals and have some action plan to achieve it accordingly.

There are some thing which are important to remember .

So, there was an ancient Indian sage who was teaching his student the art of archery. He put the wooden bird as target and asked them to aim at eye of bird . then the first student was asked that what he saw . he said that, " I saw the tress, the branches, the leaves, the sky, the bird and its eye." Then the sag said to him to wait.

Then the same question was asked by the sage to second student then he replied ,"I only saw the eye of bird."

Sage said, "Very good, then shot."

The arrow went straight and hit into eye of bird.

Now the learning from this is "unless we focus on our goals we cannot achieve them." Now many of us try very hard still sometimes we don't get success why is it ?

I have seen many peoples who have tried hard and still don't get success but some even don't try very hard and then also they get success this is because hard work should achievement but only when coupled with efficient and appropriate methods you put for doing your task.

XIV
Confidence

Confidence is a belief in oneself, the conviction that one has the ability to meet life's challenges and to succeed—and the willingness to act accordingly. Being confident requires a realistic sense of one's capabilities and feeling secure in that knowledge.

Confidence is not an innate, fixed characteristic. It's an ability that can be acquired and improved over time.

Social confidence can be developed by practicing in social settings. Individuals can observe the structure and flow of any conversation before jumping in, and they can prepare questions or topics to discuss ahead of time.

Anxiety can take hold when people are plagued by self-doubt, so putting themselves in and getting accustomed to the specific situation they fear can assure people that nothing truly bad will happen. And the activity gets easier with practice.

Outside of a social context, one can gain a sense of confidence from personal and professional accomplishments. Continuing to set and meet goals can enable the belief that one is competent and capable.

Imagine you're in the market for a new job. You've tough competition, but one of your strengths is your confidence – in yourself and your abilities. Your positive mindset sets you apart from the other applicants during interviews, and when it comes down to it, your confidence alone gives you an edge over other qualified people.

This isn't just a hypothetical scenario: studies have shown that people who believe in themselves are more likely to compete against others for the same career opportunities. Moreover, confident workers are more likely to be promoted than their less confident colleagues if they get the job.

People with high self-confidence tend to have better emotional health than those with low self-confidence. The way they think affects every aspect of their lives, including how they handle potentially stressful situations such as conflicts with colleagues and superiors or setbacks in general (whether personal or professional).

Because confident people are convinced of their abilities, they can face challenges and overcome them successfully – something that's very difficult for people who don't believe in themselves.

Fear in itself isn't a bad thing – it's a normal, healthy emotion that can help you survive dangerous situations. But it can be debilitating when it dominates your entire life and prevents you from doing what you want to do.

Don't give up. Not everything in life is geared toward success, but nothing great was ever accomplished without trying again and again until it worked out.

Avoid negative self-talk. It can be hard not to beat yourself up when things don't go as planned, but berating yourself won't get you anywhere. Instead, focus on what you did well, and what you can do better next time (with confidence!).

A person who's confident:

- has high self-esteem

- is willing to take healthy risks

- can handle criticism without feeling the need to defend themselves or be defensive of others

- takes responsibility for their own decisions and actions (rather than blaming circumstances or other people)

- understands the difference between healthy assertiveness and unhealthy aggression (I'm not talking about violence here)

-

is able to communicate her feelings appropriately (without losing control)

If you're confident, you can make the best of a bad situation. When things don't go your way, it's easy to lose hope or put yourself down. But if you've self-confidence, even when things aren't going well, you can't lose your courage and keep working toward your goals.

For example, one of your goals is to write an article for the Huffington Post. You start writing the article and think it's going pretty well until one morning you wake up and find a link to an article in the Huffington Post that says exactly what your article said!

Now you feel discouraged about this whole writing project: what's the point of writing an article if someone else has already written a similar article? But even if someone steals your idea and publishes it first, there are still ways to write an interesting article based on those ideas (even though they may no longer be original).

Confident people are more likely to get a promotion because they approach their job with a can-do attitude. They have confidence in their skills and abilities, don't mind trying new things, and accept responsibility for their work and actions.

Confidence is often a core part of professional development. The amount of professional experience is an important factor, but it is not the only one.

They aren't afraid of making mistakes because they know that mistakes are an inevitable part of learning new skills. If they don't know something, they are willing to ask for help and admit that they need more training.Develop confidence in yourself. One way to build your confidence is to engage in activities you're good at and enjoy. When you're comfortable with your abilities, new skills will come easily to you, and old ones will be easier to master.Be willing to accept constructive criticism. You learn much more from people who help you improve than from those who yell at you when they think you've failed.Admit when you don't know something and ask for help to figure it out. You may be surprised at how much knowledge someone else has that can help you solve your problem. Stay humble by admitting your mistakes and trying again when needed, rather than giving up on the first try.

Taking risks is an important part of your confidence. If you're willing to try new things, you can discover hidden talents, meet new people, and see what the world has to offer.

Self-confidence lets you know that it's okay to try something new because you accept yourself and trust that your abilities will help you through all of life's experiences. You won't be able to become the person you want to be if you don't take risks or follow your dreams. And if a risk doesn't work out, you can learn many lessons from each experience that will make life more interesting.

But that doesn't mean that self-confident people are reckless or careless – they're just not afraid to put themselves out there to grow as a person and succeed in all areas of their lives. Even when things don't go the way they were planned, they find a way to keep moving forward and achieve their goals in life.Self-confidence can have a contagious effect. When people feel confident in social situations, others are attracted to them, because confidence is magnetic: it inspires confidence in others. This is human nature: we imitate what we see and hear from other people. When someone exudes confidence, it's likely that those who observe it'll mimic their behavior.

Self-confidence helps you overcome fears and obstacles. Whether you're afraid to ask for a raise or talk about yourself at a job interview, confidence helps you push through and be on your best behavior.

With confidence, you can take more risks with less delay. It helps you try new things without thinking too much about them or wondering what could go wrong because you know that no matter what happens, you can handle it if you need to. Self-confidence leads to other people liking being around you. This is also true for potential employers who're looking for someone who's that certain something they need on their team!

How to Boost Your Confidence Levels, Including Practicing Self-Compassion, Accepting Compliments, and Setting Realistic Goals

Self-compassion is essentially treating yourself as you would treat a friend, in a nonjudgmental way. Self-compassion also involves not judging yourself when you make mistakes, but rather viewing them as opportunities to learn and grow.

Practicing self-compassion will help anyone suffering from low confidence and low self-esteem.

- Take care of yourself and your needs. While this may seem obvious, it's easy to forget that if you don't take care of yourself first, you can't effectively be there for others.

- Learn from your mistakes. Don't dwell on things that went wrong; focus instead on what went right and how to improve for next time.

- Do things that make you feel good about yourself – anything from reading, and learning a new skill to exercising.

- Put yourself in challenging situations, such as job interviews or social gatherings with people you don't know very well yet. Confidence flows from experience – it flourishes with it, in fact.

- Learn to let go of negative thoughts by distancing yourself from these thoughts So they have less power over your life.

- Trust your strong sense of what is right for you.

- Have a belief in yourself.

Use positive affirmations if they are helpful.

The more confident you become, the more you'll be able to calm the voice inside you that says, "I can't do it." You'll be able to unhook from your thoughts and take action in line with your values.

If you've suffered from low self-confidence, you're probably familiar with rumination, or the tendency to mull over worries and perceived mistakes, replaying them ad nauseam. Excessive rumination is linked to both anxiety and depression, and it can make us withdraw from the world. But by filling up your tank with confidence, you'll be able to break the cycle of over-thinking and quiet your inner critic.

Building confidence means taking small steps that leave a lasting sense of accomplishment. If you've ever learned a language, mastered a skill, reached a fitness goal, or otherwise overcome setbacks to get to where you wanted to be, you're well on your way.

You might be thinking, "Well, sure, I was proud of my 'A' in Calculus back in high school, but what does that have to do with anything now?" If you think back to a key accomplishment in your life, you'll likely find that it took a lot of perseverance. If you could triumph through adversity then, you can do it in other areas of your life where you feel self-doubt.

As your confidence grows, you'll find yourself more driven to stretch your abilities. "What-if" thoughts will still arise: "What if I fail?" "What if I embarrass myself?" But with self-assurance, those thoughts will no longer be paralyzing. Instead, you'll be able to grin and act anyway, feeling energized by your progress in pursuing goals that mean something to you.

Confidence gives you the skills and coping methods to handle setbacks and failure. Self-confidence doesn't mean you won't sometimes fail. But you'll know you can handle challenges and not be crippled by them. Even when things don't turn out anywhere close to what you planned, you'll be able to avoid beating yourself up.

As you keep pushing yourself to try new things, you'll start to truly understand how failure and mistakes lead to growth. An acceptance that failure is part of life will start to take root. Paradoxically, by being more willing to fail, you'll actually succeed more — because you're not waiting for everything to be 100 percent perfect before you act.

XV

10 inspirational short stories

1. secret of success

Once a young man asked the wise man, Socrates, the secret to success. Socrates patiently listened to the man's question and told him to meet him near the river the following day for the answer. So the next day, Socrates asked the young man to walk with him towards the river. As they went in the river, the water got up to their neck. But to the young man's surprise, Socrates ducked him into the water.

The young man struggled to get out of the water, but Socrates was strong and kept him there until the boy started turning blue. Finally, Socrates pulled the man's head out of the water. The young man gasped and took a deep breath of air. Socrates asked, 'What did you want the most when your head was in the water?" The young man replied, "Air." Socrates said, "That is the secret to success. When you want success as badly as you wanted the air while you were in the water, then you will get it. There is no other secret."

moral=A burning desire is the starting point of all accomplishment. Just like a small fire cannot give much heat, a weak desire cannot produce great results.

2. The coldest winter

It was one of the coldest winters, and many animals were dying because of the cold. The porcupines, realizing the situation, decided to group together to keep each other warm. This was a great way to protect themselves from the cold and keep each of them warm, but the quills of each one wounded their closest companions.

After a while, they decided to distance themselves, but they too began to die due to cold. So they had to make a choice: either accept the quills of their companions or choose death. Wisely, they decided to go back to being together. They learned to live with a few wounds caused by their close relationship with their companions to receive the warmth of their togetherness. This way, they were able to survive.

3. goals without meaning

A farmer had a dog who used to wait by the roadside for vehicles to come. As soon as one came, he would run down the road, barking and trying to overtake the car. One day the farmer's neighbor asked the farmer, "Do you think the dog is ever going to overtake those vehicles?" The farmer replied, "That is not what bothers me. What bothers me is what he would do if he ever caught one."

Many people in life behave like that dog who is pursuing meaningless goals.

4. A lesson in giving

Many years ago, when I worked as a transfusion volunteer at a hospital, I got to know a little three-year-old girl suffering from a disease. The little girl needed blood from her five-year-old brother, who had miraculously survived the same condition. The boy had developed the antibodies needed to combat the illness and was the only hope for his sister.

The doctor explained the situation to the little brother and asked if the boy would give his blood to his sister. I saw him hesitate only for a moment before he took a deep breath and said, "Yes, I will do it if it will save my sister."

As the transfusion progressed, he lay in bed next to his sister and smiled, seeing the color returning to her cheeks. Then his face grew pale, and his smile faded. Finally, he looked up at the nurse beside him and asked with a trembling voice, "When will I start to die?"

The young boy had misunderstood the doctor and thought he had to die to save his sick sister.

5. Unnecessary Doubts

A boy and a girl were playing together. The boy had a collection of beautiful marbles. The girl had some candies with her. The boy offered to give the girl all his marbles in exchange for all her candies. The girl agreed. The boy gave all the marbles to the girl but secretly kept the biggest and the most beautiful marble for himself. The girl gave him all her candies as she had promised. That night, the girl slept peacefully. But the boy couldn't sleep as he kept wondering if the girl had hidden some more tasty candies from him the way he had hidden his best marble.

Moral: If you don't give your hundred percent in a relationship, you'll always keep doubting if the other person has given their hundred percent.

6.The reflections

Once a dog ran into a museum filled with mirrors. The museum was unique; the walls, the ceiling, the doors and even the floors were made of mirrors. Seeing his reflections, the dog froze in surprise in the middle of the hall. He could see a whole pack of dogs surrounding him from all sides, from above and below.The dog bared his teeth and barked all the reflections responded to it in the same way. Frightened, the dog barked frantically; the dog's reflections imitated the dog and increased it many times. The dog barked even harder, but the echo was magnified. The dog, tossed from one side to another while his reflections also tossed around snapping their teeth.The following day, the museum security guards found the miserable, lifeless dog, surrounded by thousands of reflections of the lifeless dog. There was nobody to harm the dog. The dog died by fighting with his own reflections.

Moral: The world doesn't bring good or evil on its own. Everything that is happening around us reflects our thoughts, feelings, wishes and actions. The world is a big mirror. So let's strike a good pose!

7. The Old Carpenter

A carpenter with years of experience was ready to retire. He communicated with his contractor about his plans to leave the house-building business to live a more leisurely retired life with his wife and family. The contractor felt a little upset that his excellent and experienced carpenter was leaving the job, but he requested the carpenter to build just one more house for him.

The carpenter agreed with the contractor, but his heart was not in his work like it used to be. He resorted to shoddy craftmanship and used inferior materials for building the last house of his career. It was an unfortunate way to end his career. When the carpenter completed the house and the employer came to inspect the home.

He looked around the house, and just before he exited the house, he handed the front-door key to the carpenter. "This is your house," he said, "my gift to you." This was a massive surprise to the carpenter. Although it was supposed to be a good surprise, he wasn't feeling good as he felt a deep shame inside him. If he had only known he was building his own house, he would have done it all so differently. Now he had to live in a home that wasn't built that well.

Moral: Like the carpenter, we build our lives in a distracted way, reacting rather than acting, willing to put up with less rather than the best. Give your best. Your attitudes and the choices you make today will be your life tomorrow; build it wisely.

8. Build like a Child

On a warm summer at a beautiful beach, a little boy on his knees scoops and packs the sand with plastic shovels into a bucket. He upends the bucket on the surface and lifts it. And, to the delight of the little architect, a castle tower is created. He works all afternoon spooning out the moat, packing the walls, and building sentries with bottle tops and bridges with Popsicle sticks. Finally, with his hours of hard work on the beach, a sandcastle will be made.

In a big city with busy streets and rumbling traffic, a man works in an office. He shuffles papers into stacks, delegates assignments, cradles the phone on his shoulder and punches the keyboard with his fingers. He juggles with numbers, contracts get signed and much to the delight of the man, a profit is made. All his life, he will work. He was formulating the plans and forecasting the future. His annuities will be sentries, and Capital gains will be bridged. An empire will be built.

The two builders of the two castles have very much in common. They both shape granules into grandeurs. They both make something beautiful out of nothing. They both are very diligent and determined to build their world. And for both, the tide will rise, and the end will come. Yet, that is where the similarities cease. The little boy sees the end of his castle while the man ignores it. As the dusk approaches and the waves near, the child jumps to his feet and begins to clap as the waves wash away his masterpiece. There is no sorrow. No fear. No regret. He is not surprised; he knew this would happen. He smiles, picks up his tools and takes his father's hand, and goes home. The man in his sophisticated office is not very wise like the child. As the wave of years collapses on his empire, he is terrified. He hovers over the sandy monument to protect it. He tries to block the waves with the walls he made. He snarls at the incoming tide. "It's my castle," he defies. The ocean need not respond. Both know to whom the sand belongs.

Go ahead and build your dreams, but build with a child's heart. When the sun sets, and the tides take – applaud. Salute the process of life and go home with a smile.

9.Changing Vision

There once lived a wealthy man who was bothered by severe eye pain. He consulted many physicians, but none could treat his ache. He went through a myriad of treatment procedures, but his pain persisted with more vigor. He looked for every available solution for his pain and approached a wise monk renowned for treating various illnesses. The monk carefully observed the man's eyes and offered a very peculiar solution.

The monk told the man to concentrate only on the green color for a few weeks and avoid other colors. The man was desperate to get rid of the pain and was determined, ready to go to any extent. The wealthy man appointed a group of painters, purchased green paint barrels and directed that every object, his eye was likely to fall to be painted green.

After a few weeks, the monk came to visit the man to follow up on the man's progress. As the monk walked towards the man's room, the appointed painter poured a bucket of green paint on the monk. The monk could see that the whole corridor and the room were painted green. As the monk inquired about the reason for painting everything green, the wealthy man said that he was only following the monk's advice to look at only green.

Hearing this, the monk laughed and said, "If only you had purchased a pair of green spectacles worth just a few dollars, You could have saved a large share of your fortune. You cannot paint the world green."

Moral: Let us change our vision, and the world will appear accordingly.

10. Waiting for rabbit suicide

Once there lived a lazy farmer who did not enjoy working hard in the fields. He spent his days napping under a tree. One day, while he was resting under a tree, a fox came chasing a rabbit. There was a loud THUMP–the rabbit had crashed into the tree and died.

The farmer picked up the dead rabbit and took it home, frustrating the hell out of the fox. The farmer cooked and ate the rabbit for dinner and sold its fur at the market. The farmer thought to himself, "If I could get a rabbit-like that every day,

I'd never have to work again."

The next day, the farmer went right back to the tree and waited for another rabbit to die similarly. He saw a few rabbits, but none of them ran into the tree-like before. Indeed, it was a very rare incident, but the farmer did not realize it. "Oh well," he thought cheerfully, "There's always tomorrow." Since he was just waiting for the rabbit to hit a tree and die, he did not give any attention to his field. Weeds grew in his rice field. Soon, the farmer had to be hungry as he ran out of his rice and never caught any other rabbit too.

Moral: Do not wait for good things to come without doing anything. Do not give your life to luck without working for success.

11.Start with yourself

The following words were written on the tomb of an Anglican Bishop in the Crypts of Westminster Abbey:

When I was young and free, and my imagination had no limits, I dreamed of changing the world. As I grew older and wiser, I discovered the world would not change, so I shortened my sights somewhat and decided to change only my country. But it, too, seemed immovable. As I grew into my twilight years, in one last desperate attempt, I settled for changing only my family, those closest to me, but alas, they would have none of it. And now, as I lie on my deathbed, I suddenly realize: If I had only changed my life first, then by example, I would have changed my family.

From their inspiration and encouragement, I would then have been able to better my country, and who knows, I may have even changed the world.

XVI
poem

लहरों से डर कर नौका पार नहीं होती |
कोशिश करने वालों की हार नहीं होती ||
    नन्हीं चींटी जब दाना लेकर चलती है |
चढ़ती दीवारों पर, सौ बार फिसलती है ||

मन का विश्वास रगों में साहस भरता है |
चढ़कर गिरना, गिरकर चढ़ना न अखरता है ||

आख़िर उसकी मेहनत बेकार नहीं होती |
कोशिश करने वालों की हार नहीं होती ||
    डुबकियां सिंधु में गोताखोर लगाता है |
जा जाकर खाली हाथ लौटकर आता है ||

मिलते नहीं सहज ही मोती गहरे पानी में |
बढ़ता दुगना उत्साह इसी हैरानी में ||

मुट्ठी उसकी खाली हर बार नहीं होती |
कोशिश करने वालों की हार नहीं होती ||
    असफलता एक चुनौती है, स्वीकार करो |
क्या कमी रह गई, देखो और सुधार करो ||

जब तक न सफल हो, नींद चैन को त्यागो तुम |

संघर्ष का मैदान छोड़ मत भागो तुम ||

कुछ किये बिना ही जय जयकार नहीं होती |
कोशिश करने वालों की हार नहीं होती ||

XVII

Dr. Kalam was born in a poor family, to say the least. His father was a boatman and his mother, a housewife. Income was not very high, but the family was humble enough. They were five siblings, making it even difficult to make the ends meet. Dr. Kalam was the youngest but responsible enough; he decided to work at the tender age of eight. In his school years, Kalam had average grades but was described as a bright and hardworking student who had a strong desire to learn. He spent hours on his studies, especially mathematics.

He used to collect newspapers from the station and distribute them in the morning after attending maths tuition at 4 AM. Afterward, he used to attend school and then collect the dues for the newspapers in the evening. Life was tough for him since his childhood but he was always positive and motivated, especially for his studies.

While in his college, Dr. Kalam had to face the first-ever failure in his life. While working on an important project, the principal decided to check up on his progress suddenly. The principal felt dissatisfied as he had expected more than delivered. He then gave an ultimatum to Dr. Kalam; if the project could not be redone within 3 days, he would lose his scholarship. He found himself in a deep fix because not only was it difficult to be done in 3 days, but he could not afford to lose his scholarship. But he worked day and night, skipped meals, and somehow managed to finish it within the time limit.

Dr. A.P.J. Abdul Kalam's first major project at ISRO was the SLV-3 which had failed in 1979 when it had been launched for the first time. He gave a motivational speech after this incident in which he talked about the role of a team leader and how to handle success and failure. "When failure occurred, the leader of the organization owned that failure. When success came, he gave it to his team. The best management lesson I have learned did not come to me from reading a book; it came from that experience,"

A year later, in 1980, he re-launched the SLV-3, successfully. Thereafter, he launched various missiles and became the 'Missile Man' of India. Elected as the President of India in 2002, with the support of both the ruling party as well as the opposition, he served till 2007. He was always a humble and a down to earth person.

Life as that of Dr. APJ Abdul Kalam inspires the readers to learn from failures. That is what our motive at Failure Before Success is. Failures are as important as our successes, if not more; because they come with lessons that may change our outlook on life. Life is anything but a cakewalk. It is a constant journey through paths lined with thorns that eventually lead us to our destinations if we don't quit. Having high ambitions in life is easy but making them our realities require immense hard work, often through a lot of struggles. This blog is about a personality, whose life always oscillated between failing, trying hard to succeed, and succeeding, eventually.

XVIII

Kalam spoke with India Knowledge at Wharton

APJ Abdul Kalam was among India's best-known scientists before he became the country's President. An alumnus of the Madras Institute of Technology, he worked for the Indian Space Research Organisation (ISRO) where he helped launch India's first satellites into orbit. Later, Kalam worked on developing missiles and other strategic weapons; he was widely regarded as a national hero for leading India's nuclear weapons tests in 1998. In 2002, Kalam was named the country's President, and he held that position until 2007. During the Wharton India Economic Forum in Philadelphia, Kalam spoke with India Knowledge at Wharton about his career as a scientist, his vision for India's future, and the most important traits for leaders, among other issues.

APJ Abdul Kalam was among India's best-known scientists before he became the country's President. An alumnus of the Madras Institute of Technology, he worked for the Indian Space Research Organisation (ISRO) where he helped launch India's first satellites into orbit. Later, Kalam worked on developing missiles and other strategic weapons; he was widely regarded as a national hero for leading India's nuclear weapons tests in 1998. In 2002, Kalam was named the country's President, and he held that position until 2007. During the Wharton India Economic Forum in Philadelphia, Kalam spoke with India Knowledge at Wharton about his career as a scientist, his vision for India's future, and the most important traits for leaders, among other issues. An edited transcript of the interview follows:

India Knowledge at Wharton: Since our publication is called Knowledge at Wharton, could you tell us something about knowledge?

Kalam: I've written a four-line, poem-like thing called "Creativity." It goes like this: "Learning gives creativity. Creativity leads to thinking. Thinking provides knowledge. Knowledge makes you great." I have made at least a million children repeat these lines. I am very happy that Wharton has created Knowledge at Wharton; it's a beautiful idea. My greetings to all of you.

India Knowledge at Wharton: Perhaps we could begin by talking about your own past. You were born in Rameswaram in 1931. What are the biggest differences between India as it was then and India today?

Kalam: Since then I have orbited the sun 76 times. I have seen when I was a young boy the Second World War coming to an end, and the effect of war and injuries. I saw India attain her freedom in August 1947; I saw the economic ascent phase of India [beginning in] 1991. I have worked with visionaries like Prof. Vikram Sarabhai. I have seen the green revolution, the white revolution, and the telecom revolution; I have also seen the growth of information and communication technologies

(ICT), as well as India's successes in the space program and self-sufficiency in strategic weaponry. These are some of the things I have witnessed. Of course, we have a long way to go. Since we have to bring smiles to the faces of more than one billion people, we have many challenges ahead.

India Knowledge at Wharton: After studying aeronautics at the Madras Institute of Technology, you were one of India's top scientists at the Defense Research and Development Organisation (DRDO) and then at the Indian Space Research Organisation (ISRO). You helped launch several successful missiles, which led to your getting the nickname, "Missile Man." What challenges were involved in getting this program going and leading it successfully?

Kalam: I worked for ISRO for about 20 years. My team and I worked to put India's first satellite into space. Then our team took up the Integrated Guided Missile Development Program. These were youthful teams that worked with me, and they have gone on to take up much larger projects. These in turn have led to great value addition in areas such as technology, infrastructure and, above all, human resources.

One of the important lessons I learned in the space and missile program was not just how to handle success but how to deal with failure. Wharton is in the management environment. I would like young people to understand how they should manage failure. In any project you take up, you will face problems. These problems should not become the captain of the project chief; the project chief should be the captain of the problems and defeat the problems.

India Knowledge at Wharton: You were actively involved in India's nuclear weapons tests in 1998. Could you tell us about that experience and the lessons you learned?

Kalam: The main lesson I learned was how multiple technical teams and departments of the government of India could work together for a great mission as an industrial partnership. It was a great experience.

India Knowledge at Wharton: You are known to be deeply spiritual. Did you ever feel conflicted, or guilty, about developing missiles and nuclear weapons? Why, or why not?

Kalam: I realize that for my country's development, peace is essential. Peace comes from strength — because strength respects strength. That is how our weaponized missiles were born. You need strength to keep the nation peaceful, so that you can focus on the necessary developmental missions. That is how I see it.

India Knowledge at Wharton: How did you come to become India's President in July 2002? What leadership qualities does one need to lead a country as large, complex and chaotic as India?

Kalam: Well, I won't call India chaotic, because order comes from disorder. That is what is happening now.

I was elected President of India — from 2002 to 2007 — through a well-structured election process. Any leadership — whether it is political leadership or leadership in technology — requires that the leader have six traits. What are these traits?

First, the leader must have vision. Without vision, you cannot be a leader. Second, the leader must be able to travel into an unexplored path. Normally the tendency is for people to travel along well-laid out ways. Third, the leader must know how to manage success, and even more importantly, failure.

India Knowledge at Wharton: Could you give an example, from your own experience, of how leaders should manage failure?

Kalam: Let me tell you about my experience. In 1973 I became the project director of India's satellite launch vehicle program, commonly called the SLV-3. Our goal was to put India's "Rohini" satellite into orbit by 1980. I was given funds and human resources — but was told clearly that by 1980 we had to launch the satellite into space. Thousands of people worked together in scientific and technical teams towards that goal.

By 1979 — I think the month was August — we thought we were ready. As the project director, I went to the control center for the launch. At four minutes before the satellite launch, the computer began to go through the checklist of items that needed to be checked. One minute later, the computer program put the launch on hold; the display showed that some control components were not in order. My experts — I had four or five of them with me — told me not to worry; they had done their calculations and there was enough reserve fuel. So I bypassed the computer, switched to manual mode, and launched the rocket. In the first stage, everything worked fine. In the second stage, a problem developed. Instead of the satellite going into orbit, the whole rocket system plunged into the Bay of Bengal. It was a big failure.

That day, the chairman of the Indian Space Research Organization, Prof. Satish Dhawan, had called a press conference. The launch was at 7:00 AM, and the press conference — where journalists from around the world were present — was at 7:45 AM at ISRO's satellite launch range in Sriharikota [in Andhra Pradesh in southern India]. Prof. Dhawan, the leader of the organization, conducted the press conference himself. He took responsibility for the failure — he said that the team had worked very hard, but that it needed more technological support. He assured the media that in another year, the team would definitely succeed. Now, I was the project director, and it was my failure, but instead, he took responsibility for the failure as chairman of the organization.

The next year, in July 1980, we tried again to launch the satellite — and this time we succeeded. The whole nation was jubilant. Again, there was a press conference. Prof. Dhawan called me aside and told me, "You conduct the press conference today."

I learned a very important lesson that day. When failure occurred, the leader of the organization owned that failure. When success came, he gave it to his team. The best management lesson I have learned did not come to me from reading a book; it came from that experience.

India Knowledge at Wharton: That is a great story; thank you for sharing it.

Kalam: Continuing further with the six traits, the fourth trait is that the leader should have the courage to make decisions. Fifth, the leader should have nobility in management. Every action of the leader should be transparent. And finally, the leader should work with integrity and succeed with integrity.

All the traits apply especially to the President of a country. The President continuously must be in touch with the people. The Rashtrapati Bhavan [i.e., the presidential residence in New Delhi, India's equivalent of the White House] must become the people's residence. When I was President I travelled to every state, cutting across hills, deserts, and seas. I was in touch with millions upon millions of people.

India Knowledge at Wharton: In your vision for India 2020, you envisaged that differences between the urban areas and the countryside would gradually disappear. Could you explain your concept of "PURA" and how that brings about this transformation?

Kalam: The concept of PURA — which stands for "Providing Urban amenities in Rural Areas" — is about giving a cluster of villages physical, electronic and knowledge connectivity. The idea is to empower the villagers, so that economic connectivity can emerge. We planned about 7,000 PURAs for the country — including hill PURAs, coastal PURAs and plains PURAs. I believe that connectivity is the key to bridging the rural-urban divide. The core-competence of the village will enable the production of competitive products for national and international markets. This will lead to rural enterprises which will create jobs in villages and lead to a vibrant economy in India's hinterland. That is how prosperity will emerge in the rural environment.

India Knowledge at Wharton: How can India become energy independent by 2030?

Kalam: Today fossil fuels dominate the energy sector throughout the world. The World Energy Forum predicts that in five to eight decades, the fossil fuels will run out because these sources of energy are not renewable. Also, energy costs will go up. Oil is already at $110 per barrel, and if this continues, this situation will be very tough to manage.

So I set a goal of energy independence for my country. It's a three-dimensional approach. First, we should invest in solar power. Today solar power is not economical because the efficiency of solar cells is just 15% to 20%. So we should use CNT (carbon nano tubes) composites that can increase the efficiency of solar cells to 45% or 50%. Second, we should use nuclear energy, because India has abundant thorium based nuclear reactors. This is definitely a clean solution to energy needs. The third focus area should be bio-fuels, including ethanol as well as bio diesel made from jatropha [a plant that grows in wastelands] and algae. These three initiatives can free India from dependence on fossil fuels. It will also help maintain a clean environment.

India Knowledge at Wharton: In your vision for India's future technology plays an important role. How will social grids — such as the knowledge grid, the health grid and e-governance grid — help make India a developed country?

Kalam: The idea is that the knowledge grid empowers the village citizens with skill and knowledge. The health grid brings the super-specialty healthcare that is available in the cities to the doorsteps of rural citizens. And the e-governance grid brings transparent governance to the citizens. All these grids lead to economic growth and social transformation.

India Knowledge at Wharton: During your years as India's president, what was the biggest leadership challenge that you faced and how did you overcome it?

Kalam: I returned the Office of Profit Bill to the Parliament. The reason was that I felt there was no transparent system for determining whether a post was an office of profit. That was a major decision. I studied the bill and returned it to the parliament for reconsideration. It created its own dynamic, but I felt I did the right thing.

India Knowledge at Wharton: If you could rewind and replay your years as President, what might you do differently? Is there anything you wanted to accomplish that you were unable to do?

Kalam: Last year I came up with an idea: I felt I should power the Rashtrapati Bhavan completely with solar power. For that I worked on a proposal after completing four years of my Presidential term — and at the beginning of the fifth year. But then the environmental agencies raised a lot of questions. Before I could answer them, my term ended. I would have liked the Rashtrapati Bhavan to be the first home in India to be powered completely by solar energy.

India Knowledge at Wharton: One last question — you are a gifted poet. Could you please recite some lines of your favorite poem?

Kalam: My favorite poem is "The Vision." I recited it in Parliament, and I will recite it for you.

I climbed and climbed
Where is the peak, my Lord?
I ploughed and ploughed,
Where is the knowledge treasure, my Lord?
I sailed and sailed,
Where is the island of peace, my Lord?
Almighty, bless my nation
With vision and sweat resulting into happiness.

CPSIA information can be obtained
at www.ICGtesting.com
Printed in the USA
BVHW080801140623
665881BV00014B/618

9 798889 861317